my **revisi⏻n** notes

AQA **AS** CITIZENSHIP STUDIES

Mike Mitchell

Hazel White

HODDER
EDUCATION
AN HACHETTE UK COMPANY

The Publishers would like to thank AQA for the use of past exam questions on p.28, 60 and 93.

Every effort has been made to trace all copyright holders, but if any have been inadvertently overlooked the Publishers will be pleased to make the necessary arrangements at the first opportunity.

Although every effort has been made to ensure that website addresses are correct at time of going to press, Hodder Education cannot be held responsible for the content of any website mentioned in this book. It is sometimes possible to find a relocated web page by typing in the address of the home page for a website in the URL window of your browser.

Hachette UK's policy is to use papers that are natural, renewable and recyclable products and made from wood grown in sustainable forests. The logging and manufacturing processes are expected to conform to the environmental regulations of the country of origin.

Orders: please contact Bookpoint Ltd, 130 Milton Park, Abingdon, Oxon OX14 4SB. Telephone: +44 (0)1235 827720. Fax: +44 (0)1235 400454. Lines are open 9.00a.m.–5.00p.m., Monday to Saturday, with a 24-hour message answering service. Visit our website at www.hoddereducation.co.uk

© Mike Mitchell and Hazel White 2012
First published in 2012 by
Hodder Education,
An Hachette UK Company
338 Euston Road
London NW1 3BH

Impression number   10 9 8 7 6 5 4 3 2 1
Year   2016 2015 2014 2013 2012

Cover photo © BNP Design Studio / Alamy
Illustrations by Datapage (India) Pvt. Ltd.
Typeset in cronospro-Lt 12 points by Datapage (India) Pvt. Ltd.
Printed in Spain

A catalogue record for this title is available from the British Library

ISBN 978 1444 175 301

Get the most from this book

This book will help you to revise for the AQA AS Citizenship Studies specification. It is essential to review your work, learn it and test your understanding. Tick each box when you have:

● revised and understood a topic
● tested yourself and practised the exam questions.

☑ **Tick to track your progress**

Use the revision planner on pages iv–v to plan your revision, topic by topic.

You can also keep track of your revision by ticking off each topic heading in the book. You may find it helpful to add your own notes as you work through each topic.

My revision planner

6   Introduction

Unit 1 Identity, Rights and Responsibilities

Part A: Identity	Revised	Tested	Exam ready
Chapter 1 What is a citizen and perceptions of being 'British'			
10 1.1 What is a citizen?	☐	☐	☐

6.1 Human rights

The principles of human rights ———————————— Revised ☐

In most democratic countries, the rights of citizens are held in a constitution (see page 9). If this is written down in a single document, it is known as a codified constitution. Codified constitutions are difficult to change.

However, the UK does not have a written constitution. The rights of citizens and the rules of government are all clearly known but some of

Features to help you succeed

Examiner tip

Throughout the book there are tips from the examiner to help you boost your final grade.

Typical mistakes

The examiner identifies the typical mistakes candidates make and explains how you can avoid them.

Key words

Clear, concise definitions of essential key terms are provided on the page where they appear.

Exam practice

Practice exam questions are provided for each chapter. Use them to consolidate your revision and practise your exam skills.

Now test yourself

These short, knowledge-based questions provide the first step in testing your learning. Check your answers at the back of the book.

Online

Go online to check your answers to the exam questions and try out the extra quick quizzes at www.therevisionbutton.co.uk/myrevisionnotes.

Websites

Carry out some further research and make sure you have the up-to-date information and knowledge to take into the exam.

My revision planner

6 Introduction

Unit 1 Identity, Rights and Responsibilities

		Revised	Tested	Exam ready
Part A: Identity				
Chapter 1 What is a citizen and perceptions of being 'British'				
8	1.1 What is a citizen?	☐	☐	☐
11	1.2 Is there agreement about what 'being British' means?	☐	☐	☐
13	1.3 How do individuals and groups define their identity/ identities and where are these definitions drawn from?	☐	☐	☐
Chapter 2 How socially diverse is Britain?				
16	2.1 How much change and continuity is there in migration patterns?	☐	☐	☐
18	2.2 How far can Britain be described as a multicultural society?	☐	☐	☐
20	2.3 What is stereotyping?	☐	☐	☐
Chapter 3 Prejudice, discrimination and disadvantage				
23	3.1 Prejudice and discrimination	☐	☐	☐
24	3.2 Disadvantage: how are life chances distributed among different social groups?	☐	☐	☐
26	3.3 To what extent does poverty exist in Britain?	☐	☐	☐
Chapter 4 How can discrimination and disadvantage be reduced?				
29	4.1 What steps can government take to reduce discrimination and disadvantage?	☐	☐	☐
32	4.2 How effective have anti-discrimination policies been?	☐	☐	☐
Part B: Rights and responsibilities				
Chapter 5 What are rights?				
34	5.1 Concept of a 'right' and the relationship between rights and duties	☐	☐	☐
36	5.2 Different types of rights	☐	☐	☐
Chapter 6 What rights do I have?				
39	6.1 Human rights	☐	☐	☐
42	6.2 The right to know	☐	☐	☐
44	6.3 Other rights of UK citizens	☐	☐	☐
Chapter 7 The legal framework: protecting the citizen				
47	7.1 Civil and criminal law	☐	☐	☐
49	7.2 Legal representation	☐	☐	☐
51	7.3 Alternative methods of resolving disputes	☐	☐	☐

Unit 1 Identity, Rights and Responsibilities

	Revised	Tested	Exam ready

Chapter 8 How do the courts protect my rights?

		Revised	Tested	Exam ready
54	8.1 The role of the courts	☐	☐	☐
56	8.2 The courts and the Human Rights Act	☐	☐	☐
58	8.3 Judicial Review	☐	☐	☐

Unit 2 Democracy, Active Citizenship and Participation

Part A: Making a difference

Chapter 9 Who holds power in the UK?

		Revised	Tested	Exam ready
61	9.1 The concept and nature of power	☐	☐	☐
64	9.2 Who has economic power in the UK?	☐	☐	☐
69	9.3 What is the influence of the media and how is its power controlled?	☐	☐	☐

Chapter 10 The citizen and political power in the United Kingdom

		Revised	Tested	Exam ready
73	10.1 The nature of government and its impact on the lives of citizens	☐	☐	☐
76	10.2 Local democracy	☐	☐	☐
79	10.3 What is the impact of the EU on life in the UK?	☐	☐	☐

Chapter 11 Playing your part: how the citizen can get involved and make a difference

		Revised	Tested	Exam ready
84	11.1 What does 'taking part in the democratic process' mean?	☐	☐	☐
86	11.2 Citizens and the electoral process	☐	☐	☐
90	11.3 Do pressure groups improve the democratic process?	☐	☐	☐

Chapter 12 Citizenship in action: citizens working together to bring about change

		Revised	Tested	Exam ready
94	12.1 How do citizens bring about change?	☐	☐	☐
95	12.2 What are the key factors in successful campaigning?	☐	☐	☐
97	12.3 The impact of campaigns on political decision-making and political attitudes	☐	☐	☐

Part B: Active citizenship

Chapter 13 Active citizenship skills and participation

		Revised	Tested	Exam ready
99	Becoming an informed citizen, a participating citizen, and an active citizen	☐	☐	☐

Introduction

What is covered in AS level Citizenship Studies?

AS level Citizenship Studies consists of two units:

Unit 1 CIST1: Identity, Rights and Responsibilities

Unit 2 CIST2: Democracy, Active Citizenship and Participation

The units are split up into key questions, each with two issues. In this book, each chapter covers one issue. The issues are then split further into topics, which are reflected in the headings within each chapter (see pages iv–v).

Unit 1 CIST1: Identity, Rights and Responsibilities

Key questions	Issues	Chapter	Page
What does it mean to be British?	What is a citizen and perceptions of being 'British'.	1	8
	How socially diverse is Britain?	2	16
Are we all equal citizens?	Prejudice, discrimination and disadvantage.	3	23
	How can discrimination and disadvantage be reduced?	4	29
What are my responsibilities?	What are rights?	5	34
	What rights do I have?	6	39
How are my rights protected and supported?	The legal framework: protecting the citizen.	7	47
	How do the courts protect my rights?	8	54

Unit 2 CIST2: Democracy, Active Citizenship and Participation

Key questions	Issues	Chapter	Page
Who can make a difference?	Who holds power in the UK?	9	61
	The citizen and political power in the United Kingdom.	10	73
How can I make a difference?	Playing your part: how the citizen can get involved and make a difference.	11	84
	Citizenship in action: citizens working together to bring about change.	12	94
Active citizenship skills and participation.	Becoming an informed citizen, the participating citizen, being an active citizen.	13	99

Unit 1 CIST1

Worth **40 per cent** of the total AS course

Written paper – 1 hour 15 minutes

60 marks

Source-based questions and mini-essay questions

Unit 2 CIST2

Worth **60 per cent** of the total AS course

Written paper – 1 hour 30 minutes

90 marks

Source-based question and mini-essay plus structured question on active citizenship participation. Candidates bring their Active Citizenship Profile into the exam (see page 102).

Assessment Objectives (AO)

Each examination paper is written to assess the Assessment Objectives allocated to that paper. It is therefore important to be aware of the weighting for each Assessment Objective in each Unit.

Assessment Objective			CIST1	CIST2
AO1	Knowledge and Understanding	Demonstrate knowledge and understanding of specific citizenship issues (problems, events, concepts, ideas, processes and opinions). Relate subject knowledge and understanding to citizenship issues using a range of real and topical examples.	20%	10%
AO2	Analysis and Evaluation	Analyse issues, problems and events in relation to the citizenship concepts and topics studied. Evaluate information, views, opinions, ideas and arguments and assess their validity.	10%	10%
AO3	Communication and Action	Select, organise and present relevant information and arguments clearly and logically, using specialist terminology. Construct and advocate reasoned, coherent arguments with conclusions, drawing on evidence of a candidate's own participation and actions within the study of citizenship.	10%	40%

Guide to the exam questions

Examples of the full range of question types appear in this guide in the Exam Practice questions.

Unit 1 CIST1: Identity, Rights and Responsibilities

Section A: Identity

Section A is made up of four questions. There are 30 marks available. The first two questions are compulsory and are based on a source, although you should use your own relevant knowledge as well as referring to the source. **Question 1** is worth 5 marks. **Question 2** is worth 10 marks. You are then asked to choose between **Question 3** and **Question 4**, which are essay questions. Questions 3 and 4 are both worth 15 marks.

Section B: Rights and Responsibilities

Section B is also made up of four questions, which follow the same structure as Section A. The first two questions are compulsory and are based on a source, although you should use your own relevant knowledge as well as referring to the source. **Question 5** is worth 5 marks. **Question 6** is worth 10 marks. You are then asked to choose between **Question 7** and **Question 8**, which are essay questions. Questions 7 and 8 are both worth 15 marks.

Unit 2 CIST2: Democracy, Active Citizenship and Participation

Section A: Making a Difference

Section A is made up of four questions. There are 30 marks available. The first two questions are compulsory and are based on a source, although you should use your own relevant knowledge as well as referring to the source. **Question 1** is worth 5 marks. **Question 2** is worth 10 marks. You are then asked to choose between **Question 3** and **Question 4**, which are essay questions. Questions 3 and 4 are both worth 15 marks.

Section B: Active Citizenship

Section B is made up of four questions. There are 60 marks available. You have to answer all four questions. This section is about assessing your knowledge and understanding about Active Citizenship, and assessing your own participation. For this part of the exam you are allowed to refer to your Active Citizenship Profile where you have recorded your own involvement during the course. Detailed guidance for this section can be found in Chapter 13 (see page 99).

Chapter 1 What is a citizen and perceptions of being 'British'

1.1 What is a citizen?

Definitions of citizenship

Revised

- A **citizen** is a person who is a member of a country or **state**.
- **Citizenship** is a term that means 'belonging to a state'. The **rights** of the citizen are protected by the state, but citizens also have a corresponding **responsibility** to abide by the rules of the state. For example, citizens have the right to choose their government via elections, but they also have a corresponding responsibility to vote in these elections.
- A passport is often viewed as a symbol of citizenship as it declares clear membership of a state. However, modern day citizenship is more complex; it is understood to be the *active participation* in the responsibilities that come with the rights that are protected by the state.

> **Citizen** – a person who is a member of a country or state.
>
> **State** – the organisations responsible for running the country and services at both local and national level.
>
> **Citizenship** – belonging to a state as a citizen; participating in a community.
>
> **Rights** – in this context, the benefits of being a citizen.
>
> **Responsibilities** – (duties) things citizens are expected to do.

The nature of citizenship, including active citizenship

Revised

'Active citizenship' is a term that is often used to describe the condition of not simply *belonging* to a state but actually *taking an active role* in the country in which a citizen lives.

There is much debate in society about the sort of 'actions' that constitute active citizenship. It is generally understood to be activity which enhances the life of the community or country in which a person lives, through participating in the rights and responsibilities that come with being a member of a state. However, there are many ways in which citizens can do this: publicly and privately; locally or nationally; within a religious community, club/association or other organisation.

> **Typical mistake**
>
> Students sometimes make the mistake of describing active citizenship as simply 'getting involved' or 'doing something' rather than supplying specific examples. Make sure that you can give specific examples of active citizenship like those shown in the table on page 9.

This table outlines the broad areas that active citizenship can cover.

Area	Private		Public		
Role	Family member	Active neighbour or friend	Employee	Employer	Volunteer
Examples	<ul><li>Raising children</li><li>Looking after a parent</li><li>Looking after a brother or sister</li><li>Looking after an elderly relative</li></ul>	<ul><li>Looking in on an elderly neighbour</li><li>Fetching shopping for someone in need</li><li>Visiting an isolated neighbour</li><li>Listening to a friend</li></ul>	<ul><li>Paying taxes</li><li>Membership of a trade union</li><li>Organising work colleagues to participate in charity activity</li></ul>	<ul><li>Paying taxes</li><li>Membership of a trade association</li><li>Sponsorship of community projects (youth groups etc.)</li></ul>	<ul><li>Helping in a charity shop</li><li>Reading with children at a local school</li><li>Political campaigning (e.g. a group that campaigns to prevent a new town by-pass)</li><li>Membership of a parish council</li></ul>

There are no rules about how much or how little active citizenship a citizen should undertake. It is important to know that it need not be unpaid and can take varying amounts of a citizen's time. It could simply involve an employee paying taxes or it could be demonstrated by an unemployed person actively looking for work.

Citizens in modern society: citizens as subjects

Revised ☐

The term 'citizen' implies that a person is part of a **democracy** and has a say in their government. The term 'subject' describes someone who is directly controlled by a monarch. As Britain is both a democracy and has a monarch, there has been some debate about whether those living in Britain are 'citizens' or 'subjects'.

For several hundred years, the UK has had a **constitutional monarchy** which means that Parliament has the power to make laws, even though the monarch remains the head of state. British citizens elect representatives to sit in Parliament and make laws on their behalf – this can be described as a democracy. Citizens are also able to question laws and government decisions via the courts system and enjoy rights which are protected by law.

Other countries follow similar systems but Britain is different because it does not have a clear **constitution** which sets out the powers of the monarch and Parliament. As head of state, the Queen must assent (agree) to all laws that have been created in Parliament before they can be passed into law. In theory, this means that people living in Britain are technically subjects of the Queen, although they enjoy the rights and democratic powers of citizens.

> **Democracy** – a system of government in which citizens are able to influence government decisions.
>
> **Constitutional monarchy** – a form of government in which a monarch recognises Parliament as the chief law maker.
>
> **Constitution** – a set of rules that describe which institutions hold power within a state.

Differing views of citizenship

People will always disagree about what citizenship is or should be. The difference in the perception of citizenship can be separated into two main viewpoints: individualist and communitarian.

Individualist	Communitarian
Citizens have rights which allow them freedom to do as they choose within the law.	Citizens have rights; but also responsibilities to wider society.
Citizens have an obligation to follow the rules and laws of the state but have no other responsibilities/duties.	Citizens should abide by their responsibilities and duties because it helps to unite society and makes it stronger.
Citizens should have minimal impact on the lives of each other because individuals make the best decisions for themselves.	Citizenship requires an active contribution from citizens working together, as it ensures government is held to account and therefore does a better job.

Citizens' rights and duties

Britain is described as a 'liberal society' or 'liberal democracy'. This means that every citizen has equal access to specific rights, and with those rights come corresponding responsibilities or duties. These rights can generally be categorised as legal, social, moral and political.

Sociologist T H Marshall described the changing nature of British citizenship and the development of citizens' rights in three stages:

> **Welfare state** – the term used to describe a system whereby a government taxes citizens in order to provide social services and benefits to those that need them.

Stage 1 Civil rights
Early stage of development of citizens' rights in the 1700s and 1800s. Citizens were assured basic rights like freedom of speech, the right to a fair trial, freedom to practise any religion and the right to own property.

Stage 2 Political rights
During the 1800s and early 1900s, political decisions began to involve larger numbers of people and organisations. By 1928, all women and men over 21 had the right to vote. Increasing numbers of people joined trade unions or other political organisations.

Stage 3 Social and moral rights
During the mid-1900s, rights concerning the general welfare of citizens began to evolve. These included rights surrounding access to healthcare, decent housing, unemployment support and education – these rights are often described as forming the **welfare state**. There continues to be widespread debate about the levels of welfare support the state should provide. There has also been debate surrounding further rights for citizens, for example the right for a citizen to end their own life, and the rights of prisoners.

Now test yourself

1 What is the difference between the terms 'citizen' and 'subject'?
2 Explain what is meant by the term 'active citizenship'.
3 Why do people differ in their definition of citizenship?
4 Outline an example of each of the following: civil right, political right, social right.

Answers on p.104

1.2 Is there agreement about what 'being British' means?

The nature of British citizenship

Revised

The table below outlines the main categories of British citizenship status:

British citizen	British Overseas Territories Citizenship (BOTC)	Types of citizenship status for peoples in former colony countries	Dual citizenship	British citizens and citizenship of the European Union (EU)
The most common type of citizenship status. Automatic full citizenship rights (including the right to live, work and vote in UK).	Since 2002, people living in these existing territories (e.g. Gibraltar) have full British citizenship rights. Automatic full citizenship rights.	Before the 1960s, most people from former British colonies (e.g. India) were given the right to adopt British citizenship. During the 1980s, controls were tightened on this type of British citizenship.	People that leave Britain and are adopted by another nation can still maintain their British citizenship. The same is true for many people leaving other countries to adopt British citizenship.	The UK is one of 27 members of the European Union – EU citizens also have rights to travel, work and live, vote, stand for election and be protected by law anywhere in the EU.

Typical mistake

Students sometimes get confused about what is meant by the terms 'Britain', 'Great Britain' and the 'United Kingdom (UK)'. See key terms below.

Students also need to remember that Britain still has fourteen overseas territories – this is relevant when discussing the topic of immigration to the UK and also the process of becoming a British citizen.

United Kingdom of Great Britain and Northern Ireland – the state containing the countries of England, Scotland, Wales and Northern Ireland. Often abbreviated to the United Kingdom or UK. Citizens of this state are known as British citizens.

Great Britain – the island encompassing the territories of England, Scotland and Wales; also known as Britain.

British Overseas Territories – fourteen territories of the United Kingdom which fall under its jurisdiction; the remnants of the British Empire. Examples are Gibraltar, the Falkland Islands and Bermuda.

Becoming a British citizen

The table below outlines the main ways a person may become a British citizen.

> **Websites**
>
> Information from the Border Agency on British Citizenship: www.ukba.homeoffice.gov.uk/britishcitizenship

> **Culture** – the usual customs or beliefs of a group of people with shared heritage or history.

Born in UK	A person automatically becomes a British citizen if they are: ● born in the UK, and ● their parents are married, and ● at least one of their parents is a British citizen. If their parents are not married, then the child becomes a British citizen if the mother is a British citizen or settled in UK.
Adoption	A child adopted by a British citizen becomes a British citizen on the day of adoption order.
Descent	A child who is born outside the UK but has a British parent becomes a British citizen as long as their parent didn't acquire citizenship by descent (e.g. their parents were British but did not live in the UK).
Registration	A child born in the UK that is not registered for British citizenship can qualify for citizenship at ten years of age if they have not spent more than 90 days a year outside of the UK; or if their parent becomes a British citizen.
Naturalisation	A person of another nationality can become a British citizen if: ● they have lived in Britain for five years (or three if married to a British citizen) ● they can show understanding of English, Welsh or Gaelic language and British **culture** ● they complete a language and knowledge test ● they complete an application form and pay approximately £150 ● they attend a citizenship ceremony.

The development of the UK and its constituent parts

The United Kingdom of Great Britain and Northern Ireland has developed over time into the territories as we know it today:

● In 1707, England (which included Wales and the Channel Islands) united with Scotland to form Great Britain. The new country was governed by a Parliament in Westminster with the monarch as head of state.

● In 1801, the northern part of Ireland joined the union and the United Kingdom of Great Britain and Northern Ireland was created. All members are governed by the Houses of Parliament in Westminster with the same monarch as head of state.

● In the late 1990s, *some* power was devolved or passed from the Houses of Parliament to assemblies in Scotland, Wales and Northern Ireland. This was as a result of several **referendums** in those nations. It was intended to enable decisions affecting the nations to be made in the locality.

> **Referendum** – a vote in which citizens, within a country or region, are asked to answer 'yes' or 'no' to a single important issue.

The concept of 'Englishness'

The concept of 'Englishness' remains a much contested one. The colonial history of the UK and its history of migration have meant that the population of England comprises many religions, cultures and ethnicities, with people and their families originating from many different countries. This diversity can sometimes make it difficult to identify what it means to be typically 'English'.

The fact that Britain is divided into four nations with specific identities and the regions within England also have very different cultures make the identification of common characteristics, culture and beliefs difficult. When asked to describe their national identity, some people will describe themselves as English, distinguishing themselves from citizens of the other nations in the UK, but others would give their nationality as 'British'.

The nature of British identity

Identifying what it means to be British can be problematic. National identity is a very personal concept; it may even be hard to express as any more than simply a 'feeling' or 'sense'. What makes us feel united may be as simple as a symbol (e.g. a flag, stamp or image) or it may be language, accent or dialect.

The royal family is often cited as a unifying emblem of 'Britishness', but conversely, many view the monarchy as outdated and not at all symbolic of their national identity. Particular events may signify for some what it means to be British – whether it is a moment of great joy or sadness, the nation seems suddenly united in its emotions, e.g. the joy expressed on the wedding of Prince William and Catherine Middleton, or the sadness expressed after the death of Diana Princess of Wales.

> **Examiner tip**
>
> If you are asked in the exam 'What does it mean to be British?', you must explain that it is impossible to reach a consensus, even if you yourself are very clear on your own opinion of British identity. The examiner is looking for your ability to understand that identity is a personal expression and it may be influenced by many factors.

Now test yourself

1. Describe two categories of citizenship status.
2. List three ways in which a person can become a British citizen.
3. Why is it difficult to define what it means to be British?
4. Give three examples of factors which might impact a person's sense of national identity.

Answers on p.104

1.3 How do individuals and groups define their identity/identities and where are these definitions drawn from?

The factors that influence identity are linked to the communities that citizens associate with and participate in. There is continual debate and research into the extent to which identity is formed by nature (biological aspects that mould our identity) or nurture (socially constructed aspects of our identity).

Socialisation

'Socialisation' means learning the social **norms** and **values** of a culture.

> **Norms**–socially accepted behaviour.
> **Values**–things we consider important that support our norms.

Socialisation happens from the moment we are born, where we are heavily influenced by those people who we are in frequent and direct contact with, usually family members. This stage is known as primary socialisation and is where a person learns the basics of human interaction such as language, trust and affection and the values and norms particular to their family.

Secondary socialisation begins when we communicate with others outside of our immediate family, for example, when we go to school. At this stage, we start to develop an understanding of the universal norms and values in society and learn more formal systems of communications and behaviour. During the secondary stage of socialisation we start to develop our own identity and beliefs independent of parents via what we learn from others around us, such as peer group or teachers.

Factors that influence identity — Revised

Social class	There is debate about whether differences in social class are distinct enough for it to be considered an influence on identity. Improved salary, working hours and conditions, life chances and education have meant that the traditional working class has now arguably merged into a larger middle class.
Regionality	Where an individual lives within the UK may influence how they identify themselves as it can have an impact on culture (e.g. food), and may be entwined with employment if certain areas have a history of a particular industry (e.g. mining in Wales and the North of England).
Ethnicity	Ethnicity describes a combination of a person's race and citizenship and may be key to defining an individual's heritage and nationality – especially if this also identifies a common community (e.g. Black British or White Irish).
Religion	A person's faith or being atheist (having no faith) may be a very important and personal indicator of identity. Religion will certainly have a large impact on an individual or group's norms, values and culture; and may be the influence they believe is the most important in defining their identity.
Age	Age groups often have distinct cultures – defined by their norms and values. This can mean that age may be a key aspect of an individual's identity and define their peer groups.
Gender	An individual's sex is a biological characteristic, gender is a social and cultural characteristic. It is associated with identity of different sexes – male (masculine) or female (feminine). Gender is perhaps the most fundamental influence on a person's identity.
Nationality	Citizens of a country share common features or behaviours which often make them distinct from other countries. This also means individuals are able to relate to each other in a country and share a sense of belonging and common identity. Nationality can prove a complex factor of identity as individuals may have dual nationality, or may have originated in one country but become a naturalised citizen of another.
Employment	This is increasingly used instead of social class as an indicator of culture. Employment or types of employment in distinct industries or sectors can mean that groups have a common vested (financial) interest and also similar values and norms.
Education	Whether an individual was educated in a state school (funded by the government), private school or faith school may impact their norms, values and culture. University education may also be a factor that influences identity.

Typical mistake
Make sure you are clear and distinct in your descriptions of ethnicity, race and religion. Some students confuse these three aspects of identity and their responses show a lack of understanding which is required of them.

Now test yourself

Tested ☐

1 Outline two key factors that influence a group or individual's identity.
2 What is the difference between primary and secondary socialisation?
3 Why is social class no longer seen as influential in defining identity?
4 How are issues of identity linked to the subject of citizenship?

Answers on p.104

Exam practice

Why is it so difficult to define citizenship?   (15 marks)

Answers and quick quiz online

Online ☐

Chapter 2 How socially diverse is Britain?

2.1 How much change and continuity is there in migration patterns?

Immigration and emigration

Revised

Migration is a term used to describe the movement of people from one place to another; this may involve moving within a country's borders or across national borders.

Migration has become an increasingly prominent topic as countries attempt to control their population numbers. Those already living within a country's borders often feel anxious about **immigration** as they feel the services, standard of living and culture of their country may be adversely affected. This can often cause conflict.

> **Migration** – moving away from one place to another.
>
> **Immigration** – moving into a country from another country.

Reasons why people migrate

Revised

The reasons why people migrate can be organised into push and pull factors. Push factors are the reasons why a person leaves a particular area. Pull factors are the reasons why a person moves to a particular area.

Push factors	Pull factors
Famine: People can be forced to migrate to another area because of famine caused by crop failure or conflict. They may have no option but to move in order to find food and water.	**Employment:** People move to a place that can provide more job opportunities and a higher income. It may be that moving is the only way to find employment. Those emigrating to find work tend to be young, male, either single or with young families at home, at post-education stage and in good health.
War: People flee a place because of conflict.	**Living conditions:** People move to a place that has a better standard of living – better health provision, better education or a better climate.
Natural disasters: Flooding, drought, an earthquake or a tsunami can all force people to migrate.	**Study:** Students look to gain qualifications at universities abroad.
Persecution or oppression: People may be forced to migrate as they are persecuted or oppressed on the basis of religion, political affiliation or sexuality.	**Emotional factors:** People move to be closer to family members or to be near a place of religious or cultural significance for them.

Long-term migration

Revised

The UK government defines long-term migration as lasting more than one year. Although the process of emigrating between EU countries is simple (due to the UK's membership of the European Union), immigration to the UK from non-EU countries is much more complex.

Emigration from the UK

Revised

Factors affecting emigration from the UK are often linked to foreign governments trying to recruit workers to make up for skills shortages in their countries. Australia and New Zealand's governments have both encouraged workers from the UK to **emigrate** there by offering incentives of free travel and help with housing costs.

> **Emigration** – moving out of a country to another country.

Immigration into the UK

Revised

Arguments *against* immigration to the UK	Arguments *for* immigration to the UK
Too much immigration increases population numbers too quickly. This causes problems with resources and services.	Although there are concerns about immigrants raising the overall population too rapidly, many only stay for a short time and then leave. **Net migration** is the key indicator of population increase.
Migrants are a drain on public services like education and the National Health Service.	Host governments do not have to pay for education and training of skilled migrants and most migrant workers are young and healthy. Home Office reports indicate that immigrants contribute more in taxes than they receive in services.
Migrant workers take jobs from British workers.	Skills shortages may be filled by migrant workers. Migrants may be attractive to employers because they might be willing to work for longer hours with lower wage demands. Employers often report that migrant workers are more reliable and less likely to leave the job in the short term. Migrant workers are more likely to live in temporary accommodation and therefore more likely to move around the country to fill job vacancies.

Typical mistake

Students sometimes make the mistake of portraying only one point of view, or only their own opinion, when responding to a question. The examiner is looking for your ability to demonstrate knowledge of the varying opinions around citizenship issues and analyse and evaluate their relevance and validity. If you are asked a question on opinions about immigration, make sure you include arguments for and against.

> **Net migration** – the difference between those immigrating and those emigrating, the 'in' and 'out' figures.

Trends and patterns in UK migration since 1945

Revised

The UK has a long history of immigration. Many argue that it is the mixture of nationalities and cultures that have been introduced over time that has shaped Britain to create its unique identity.

- The UK has a long history of colonial activity so now has links to many countries. This has had an effect on migration to the UK since 1945 as people in these countries have been able to claim British citizenship (see page 11).
- The Second World War (1939–1945) had a dramatic effect on migration across the world and saw those who had helped in the war effort or fought for Britain being offered British citizenship.
- After the Second World War, the UK needed to add to its workforce as so many people had been killed or injured, so it actively recruited workers from outside of its borders.
- In recent years there has been a shortage of people with experienced skills to work for the NHS and so the government encouraged nurses from outside of the UK to fill nursing posts.
- Other events or factors have also affected migration since 1945:
  - the declaration of Indian independence in 1947, when many Indian people were allowed to move to Britain
  - expulsion of Gujarati people from Uganda between 1965 and 1972 meant a large number of Gujarati people sought refuge in the UK as Uganda is a member of the British Commonwealth.
  - European Union expansion in 2004 has meant an increasing number of EU citizens have had easier movement around the EU and into the UK.

Origins and destinations

Revised

The table below shows the countries which people immigrating into the UK come *from* in the left-hand column. The right-hand column shows the countries which most people emigrating from the UK go *to*.

Estimated number of immigrants from most common destinations in 2010		Estimated number of emigrants to most common destinations in 2010	
Country of origin	Number of UK immigrants	Destination country	Number of UK emigrants
India	66,000	Australia	39,000
Pakistan	32,000	USA	24,000
Poland	30,000	France	18,000
Australia	29,000	Poland	18,000
China	29,000	Spain	15,000

Source: Office of National Statistics www.ons.gov.uk

Now test yourself

Tested

1 Identify some of the 'push' and 'pull' factors affecting migration.
2 What are some of the arguments both for and against immigration?
3 Name some events that have affected immigration to the UK since 1945.
4 What is the most common destination for those emigrating from the UK?

Answers on p.104

2.2 How far can Britain be described as a multicultural society?

The degree of social diversity in Britain

Revised

Social diversity is the variety and differences in the identities of people. It describes diversity in terms of social class, gender, age and religion. However, it is the diversity within society in terms of *ethnicity* that is crucial to the study of **multiculturalism**. It is of course a generalisation to assume that every individual from a particular ethnic group is the same. There is further diversity within ethnic groups in terms of income, region, gender, etc.

Social diversity – the variety and differences in identities of people.

Multicultural – describes a culture comprising a variety of ethnic groups, creating a collective culture.

England is the most ethnically diverse nation within the UK. This is mainly because it contains London:

- London has a wide range of jobs, both high and low skilled, and it is where many companies have their international headquarters.
- It is the centre of commerce; the 'city of London' is the financial centre of Europe.
- It has a busy dock and has historically been the initial destination of immigrants to Britain.
- It consists of more urban areas than any other city in the UK. Urban areas are much more ethnically diverse than rural areas because urban areas offer a greater chance of employment and education.

Typical mistake

Ensure that when responding to questions on multiculturalism, your answers do not make sweeping generalisations about cultural, ethnic or faith groups.

For example, assuming that 'all Muslim women wear Burkas' would be a false generalisation and demonstrates a lack of required knowledge and understanding.

Employment has traditionally drawn migrants to the UK. The types of employment they undertook tended to dictate ethnic diversity in certain areas. For example, the Pakistani community has tended to settle in areas with textiles industries, e.g. Manchester, Yorkshire, Leeds, Birmingham and Leicester.

Can Britain be described as a multicultural society? — Revised

The fact that Britain is diverse does not mean Britain is integrated. To explore how far integration has occurred we can use two different theories: the multicultural model and the assimilation model.

Multicultural model	Assimilation model
Characterised by diversity of different cultural backgrounds. All cultures are celebrated.	Individual and group diversity exist but are assimilated (absorbed) into a collective national identity.
Individuals and groups have clear identities based on their cultural and ethnic backgrounds. No one culture is considered dominant.	National identity takes precedence over individual identity; the cultural and ethnic backgrounds of immigrants become less important.
Modern Britain is described as 'multicultural' and anti-discrimination laws exist to protect cultural diversity.	Said to have existed in Britain after the Second World War.
Differences in culture, ethnicity and belief are encouraged and shared understanding of one another exists.	Each generation assimilates to become more like the destination country and less related to the country of origin.

Issues relating to living in a multicultural society — Revised

There are many contemporary issues related to living in a multicultural society. These are often in areas where there has been a significant increase in immigration.

- Resentment over migrant workers getting jobs instead of local residents.
- Lack of **ethnic integration** due to cultural differences, for example different food and language.
- Increases in race-related crime and violence.
- Non-English-speaking migrants working long hours in factories with mainly other non-English-speaking workers. Research by the Joseph Rowntree Foundation found this made it very difficult for the non-English-speaking migrants to fit into their local community.
- Policing a multicultural society – the need for interpreters, and the differences between what is considered illegal in one country but legal in another, e.g. difference in drink driving limits.

> **Ethnic integration** – different ethnic groups becoming part of one culture.

Now test yourself — Tested

1 Outline the differences between the multicultural and assimilation models of integration.
2 Explain why London is so ethnically diverse.
3 Why might urban areas be more ethnically diverse than rural areas?
4 Identify some contemporary issues relating to living in a multicultural society.

Answers on p.104

2.3 What is stereotyping?

Concepts of stereotyping and labelling

Stereotyping gives the impression that all members of a certain group behave in the same way. It often exaggerates an element of a group's identity above all other elements of their identity.

Labelling is giving individuals or groups a 'tag' or name, for example young people wearing hooded tops are often labelled as 'trouble makers'. Such labels often reflect media or public perception but this is not necessarily the reality. Some labels may be positive, e.g. 'clever' or 'good citizen', but some maybe negative and damaging, e.g. 'pervert' or 'terrorist'.

> **Stereotyping** – over-simplification or a generalised impression of a group's identity or behaviour.
>
> **Labelling** – a process of giving tags or names to behaviour and/or groups of people.

The nature of stereotypes

Some theorists believe stereotyping is a unconscious function developed by human beings to try to simplify or categorise people and the world around them – an easy way to quickly make sense of situations. Some people may fit a stereotype and others may not.

Others believe that stereotypes originate from dominant groups in society, for example that:

- the stereotyping of women as sex objects or housewives was created by men who were previously dominant in society
- the stereotyping that 'all black men play basketball' was created by dominant white generalisations about black culture.

Although to some degree making general assumptions about people is a way of understanding the social world surrounding us, it is important to remember that these assumptions may not be correct and may be informed by media bias or even prejudice. Stereotyping becomes problematic when we assume all people fit the stereotype.

> **Typical mistake**
>
> Occasionally students respond to questions on stereotyping by insisting that it is a necessary and inescapable part of human nature and the stereotypes are usually 'true' or 'proven'. Although you will be given credit for understanding that making assumptions about individuals and groups may be a subconscious function it is important that your response is clear that stereotypes are generalisations that may be based on myth, misinformation or prejudice.

The media

The media often stereotype as a means of creating typical characters that we can associate with, but again this can be problematic if it entrenches stereotypes in the minds of readers/viewers/listeners and encourages myths about those groups or causes prejudices.

Advertising	Women are often portrayed as housewives, in charge of domestic chores and childcare.
Television	TV shows can often stereotype the roles of men and women, ethnic groups and the behaviour of homosexuals – portraying men as dominant, black men as criminals and gay men as camp or promiscuous.
Newspapers	In recent times newspapers have been accused of Islamophobia – portraying young Muslim men as terrorists or potential threats.

Exam practice answers and quick quizzes at **www.therevisionbutton.co.uk/myrevisionnotes**

Role of the mass media

The **mass media** are a major influence on how we see others in society – especially those individuals or groups that we are less likely to come into contact with in our own lives. To understand how the media influences our view of stereotypes, we must understand how the media influences us in general. In the table below you will see three models of media influence.

> **Mass media** – the organisations that produce all forms of media for a vast audience.

Models of media influence

Marxist, manipulative model	Cultural dominance model	Pluralist model
Description: The mass media is used as a way of controlling workers – spreading suspicion about minority groups who might threaten the power of the wealthy in society. The mass media encourages conformity with rules of capitalist society, i.e. not deviating from the expected patterns of behaviour or beliefs of a worker.	**Description:** The mass media is an industry that is made up of a narrow range of identities, leading to a narrow range of opinion, content and imagery. Topics and **bias** of media reflect the narrow opinion and agenda of this group in society rather than the wider public. The mass media is dominated by white middle-class males educated to degree level leading to a dominant identity which creates a dominant set of stereotypes.	**Description:** The mass media is a reflection of the media we wish to consume and we don't watch/read any content that we don't want to. Content only exists because the public demand it. Should the public disagree with the bias or content of particular media, they would stop using it and find an alternative. Therefore any stereotyping within the media is merely a reflection of existing stereotyping in society.
Criticism: This model assumes that we simply receive messages from the media and believe them. Use of '**new media**' means media is increasingly interactive and content is created or impacted on by the audience. All sorts of views can be expressed and stereotypes are therefore less likely to be 'fed' to the audience.	**Criticism:** Whereas 30 years ago the cultural dominance model may have held some weight, women and those from various cultural backgrounds are increasingly represented in higher education and the media industry. It is therefore no longer justifiable to argue that male, middle-class graduates dominate the media.	**Criticism:** This model assumes that the public are not influenced by the media available and would cease to buy/watch any content with which they disagreed. It also assumes that it is the norm for the public to source information or entertainment from a wide range of sources with a wide range of owners, thus minimising the risk of bias.

> **Bias** – favouring one side over another or at the expense of another.
>
> **New media** – information that use computers or the internet, rather than traditional methods such as television and newspapers.

Examiner tip

When responding to an exam question on the role of the media in forming opinion, ensure that you refer to the different theories about how it does so, and to what extent.

Now test yourself

1 Give examples of ways in which people may stereotype and label others in society.
2 Outline some of the reasons why people may stereotype others.
3 What are some examples of the ways in which the media may stereotype groups or individuals?
4 Assess the main theories of the influence of the media on stereotyping.

Answers on p.105

Exam practice

Source: Welfare spending

As the government has cut welfare spending in difficult times, the debate has once again taken place about which individuals and social groups deserve money from the state, how much they should receive, and the extent of poverty and relative poverty. The debate is often too focused on a few cases which are not typical of welfare recipients, as they receive a lot of more money than average. For example, some families get £1500 a week for rent to live in central London.

Your answer should refer to the passage as appropriate, but you should also include other relevant information.

In what ways does the media stereotype certain social groups? **(10 marks)**

Answers and quick quiz online

Online

Examiner tip

This exam question is a short response question that links to a source. Referring to the source is helpful but totally relying upon the source will not allow you to achieve high level marks.

This question asks about the media and stereotyping. It is important that you use examples to support your response.

Possible structure:

1 Outline a range of media formats (see page 20) – are some involved in stereotyping more than others?

2 Define some groups that are subject to stereotyping.

3 Outline, using examples, how the media stereotypes some groups. Within the time available, it is better to deal with up to three examples rather than writing briefly about lots of groups.

Chapter 3 Prejudice, discrimination and disadvantage

3.1 Prejudice and discrimination

Definitions of prejudice and discrimination
Revised

Prejudice is a set of views or opinions about people or groups of people that consider them to be inferior to other groups. It may take many forms: it could be the belief that men are superior to women or white people are superior to black people.

If prejudice is acted upon and used to treat a person or group differently, then this becomes **discrimination**. Discrimination can be positive or negative, direct or indirect.

> **Prejudice** – beliefs that one group or aspect of identity is better or worse than another.
>
> **Discrimination** – acting on prejudiced beliefs, treating a person or group of people differently.

Different types of discrimination
Revised

Positive Discrimination	Sometimes called 'affirmative action', this is where an individual or group is treated differently with the intention to improve their situation, e.g. a teacher that spends more time teaching boys in a subject in which boys have historically struggled to achieve compared to girls.
Negative Discrimination	Discrimination may also be negative, with people acting on their prejudice to treat someone unfairly and the outcome is likely to cause harm or restrict an individual/group in some way, e.g. a manager that responds negatively towards a particular employee because of a prejudiced belief.
Direct Discrimination	This describes discrimination that is deliberate and obvious. This can be deliberately abusing someone or treating them unfairly, for example mocking someone because they have a disability.
Indirect Discrimination	This form of discrimination may not be deliberate but may lead to a person or group being treated differently, for example neglecting to install disabled access in a school so that disabled students cannot attend certain classes.

Typical mistake

Sometimes students can inadvertently allow their own bias to influence their response to questions on prejudice and discrimination. For example some students are opposed to any form of positive discrimination (affirmative action) and allow their response to detail why positive discrimination is a 'negative' or 'bad' thing. Remember that at A level your responses must remain neutral in their opinion and simply assess evidence impartially – weighing up relevant arguments to come to a considered conclusion.

Bases of prejudice
Revised

A person may like or dislike a particular person due to their personal preference and experience, but this does not make them prejudiced. Prejudice concerns the 'pre-judging' of a person or group based on beliefs about a group in society, often beliefs based on inaccurate information or irrational fear. That prejudice may be based on stereotypes or **xenophobia**.

> **Xenophobia** – extreme irrational fear of foreigners.

Forms of prejudice

Revised

Sexism	Describes a prejudiced view of women as inferior to men or men as inferior to women.
Racism	Prejudice based on the belief that a particular race is superior to others, and that some races are inferior to others.
Homophobia	Describes an irrational fear of homosexuality and subsequent hatred and prejudice that result from that irrational fear.
Islamophobia	Describes an irrational fear of Islam or Muslims. This is now understood as a form of racism.

Examiner tip

When responding to a question on discrimination it is important to consider, where relevant, all forms of discrimination (see page 23). Instead of simply assuming discrimination is always direct and negative, discuss indirect and positive discrimination in order to show good levels of knowledge and understanding, as well as being able to evaluate the question fully.

Forms that discrimination may take

Revised

Bullying	Bullying can occur between individuals or small groups and could lead to physical abuse. It generally encompasses harassment and intimidation.
Antilocution	This is a term which describes verbal remarks made against a person, group or community, which are not addressed directly to them. This can cause prejudices to fester and become accepted by others as they are never tackled directly; it can create an environment where discrimination is acceptable. This form of discrimination can also progress to other more serious forms.
Physical abuse	Prejudice can cause people to commit physical abuse against others. The term 'hate crimes' describes acts of violence that are perpetrated towards a victim based on their membership or perceived membership of a specific social group (e.g. defined by ethnicity, disability, nationality, religion, sexuality, etc.).
Genocide	This describes a much wider scale of discrimination against a large group of people, usually based on racial prejudice. It is perhaps the most brutal and horrific form of discrimination and is the intent to destroy a national, ethnic, racial or religious group (this can be a perceived rather than real group). It can involve mass murder, rape and torture.

Now test yourself

Tested

1 Outline four different types of discrimination.
2 Identify the difference between prejudice and discrimination.
3 How does genocide contrast with other forms of discrimination?
4 Explain three examples of the basis for prejudice.

Answers on p.105

3.2 Disadvantage: how are life chances distributed among different social groups?

The nature of life chances

Revised

Life chances, the opportunities available in life, alter throughout an individual's life as their circumstances change. Finances, health, employment opportunities and access to education may vary throughout a person's life, affecting how easy it is for them to achieve their goals or desires.

Some people may have 'lucky breaks', some may be able to utilise contacts or family members to gain opportunities, others may simply work independently until they achieve their goals.

> **Life chances** – opportunities available to individuals or social groups.

Some theorists believe that our society in Britain is meritocratic; that a citizen's life chances are defined by how hard they work and the talents they have. **Meritocracy** is the idea that each individual has a fair and equal chance to achieve their goals, so any higher status or higher pay that someone has is earned and therefore deserved or just. This assumes that everyone has equal access to opportunities.

However, some theorists believe that although everyone has access to services like education and healthcare, the quality of those services varies, so in reality individuals do *not* have equal access to opportunities. Another argument is that those with powerful positions or high status use that to secure opportunities for members of their own families (**nepotism**), giving them more opportunities than others.

> **Meritocracy** – a society in which people have power because of their abilities, not because of their money or social position.
>
> **Nepotism** – using your power or influence to get good jobs or unfair advantages for members of your own family.

Factors influencing life chances
Revised

Education	Being able to access different types of school education can dramatically affect life chances. Students that attend independent schools and grammar schools often achieve better GCSE and A level grades than those attending comprehensive state schools. This dramatically increases their chances of going on to university, and the success of their subsequent employment opportunities.
Income	Household income can have a dramatic impact on an individual's life chances. A child that comes from a low income home is less likely to have access to resources that allow them to do well at school (e.g. books, the internet) and fewer opportunities to take part in extracurricular activities.
Employment	Some areas have fewer job opportunities than others, possibly due to the decline in a particular industry or because rural areas often have fewer employment opportunities.
Health	Some people's access to healthcare varies depending on where they live; rural areas can sometimes have limited services and services in urban areas can sometimes become oversubscribed.

The relationship between life chances and other factors
Revised

Gender	Life expectancy for women is higher than for men across all social classes. The average salary for women is still significantly lower than that of men, with women often restricted to part-time and lower paid jobs because of expectations around childcare.
Social class	The children of parents in higher social classes are more likely to end up in higher social classes themselves. Research conducted by the Joseph Rowntree Foundation suggests that this remains the case even when educational achievement is taken into account.
Age	Average life expectancy is increasing which means that there are more elderly people than ever before. • As their income is likely to be from pensions or savings, which tend to be lower than average wages, many elderly people live on low incomes and are reliant on the government to protect their standard of living. • Youth tends to be valued more than experience and life skills which means elderly people often get overlooked for employment or promotion. • Elderly people are more likely to need health care services than any other group of people.
Disability	Disabled people are less likely than able bodied people to be in full-time education, employment or training. They also earn less than able bodied people who have the same qualifications or training.
Sexuality	Gay and lesbian people face significant barriers to life chances due to prejudice and discrimination. Homophobic discrimination is often a very personalised discrimination carried out on young, vulnerable and often confused people facing identity dilemmas. Facing homophobic discrimination such as bullying at school can cause significant impact on life chances.
Ethnicity	The issue of ethnicity and life chances is complex. In some respects, minority ethnic groups may have been disadvantaged financially due to migration, but some ethnic groups (Caribbeans, Black Africans, Indians and Chinese) experience greater **social mobility** than their white counterparts, which is thought to be due to educational achievement.

> **Social mobility** – the movement of individuals or groups in social position.

Social class

Traditional descriptions of social class are increasingly viewed as irrelevant. Instead sociologists look to the occupations of an individual's parents to ascertain their social class. These are defined as follows:

Level of social class	Occupations	Examples
1	Higher managerial and professional occupations	Company managing directors, senior military officers, teachers and barristers
2	Lower managerial and professional occupations	Police officers and nurses
3	Intermediate occupations	Secretaries and driving instructors
4	Small employers	Builders and taxi drivers
5	Lower supervisory, craft and related occupations	Butchers and bus drivers
6	Semi-routine occupations	Postal workers and shop assistants
7	Routine occupations	Refuse collectors and call centre operators
8	Never worked/long-term unemployed	*Not applicable*

Source: From the National Statistics Socioeconomic Classification Census 2001.

Now test yourself

1 Explain how education, health and employment can affect life chances.
2 'British society is a meritocracy.' Assess this statement.
3 What is the effect of social class and gender on life chances?
4 Identify three other factors that may affect life chances and assess their impact.

Answers on p.105

3.3 To what extent does poverty exist in Britain?

Social distribution of poverty in Britain

- Poverty means not having enough money to pay for the basics that are needed to live.
- The most frequently used measure of poverty is average household income. If a household income falls below the national average, then it is classified as a low-income household. This can be due to a household earning below-average wages, or being a non-working household due to unemployment or disability.
- Living costs affect poverty, and some households have higher living costs than others, such as families with lots of children or families with a disabled parent. However, these families would be able to claim benefits from the government, such as child benefit. Benefits help to reduce income inequality because they predominantly go to households with low incomes.
- Rural households are more likely to be low-income households as they are more likely to have below-average wages compared to those in urban areas. However, living costs are higher in urban areas so measures based on income must be done with caution.

Relative and absolute poverty

Revised

The issue of how to define poverty has been widely debated by theorists. Some argue we should disregard poverty as a term and focus on those groups who are on the lowest incomes in society. There are two broad models of defining poverty: relative poverty and absolute poverty.

Relative poverty	Defined as the lack of a socially acceptable level of resources compared with the average for any given group or society, e.g. a desk to do homework, or access to a computer, could be claimed to be vital to fully participate in society in the UK.
Absolute poverty	Defined as the lack of the very basics needed for healthy living, such as shelter, clothing, food, water, medicine and education.

The government tends to use the relative definition of poverty (rather than absolute) because few people in the UK face absolute poverty.

Explanations of the causes and consequences of poverty

Revised

Causes of poverty

Explanations about what causes poverty can be described by two different models: the structural model and the individual behaviour model.

Structural model	Individual behaviour model
This model suggests that causes of poverty are beyond the control of the individual. It says that poverty is the result of society's reluctance to help solve the problem. If the wealthy population paid more taxes, this would help pay for resources and jobs and help a community out of decline.	This model recognises that where a person lives does affect levels of poverty but argues that the individuals themselves are the cause of poverty and therefore the solution.
	According to this model, poverty is due to an individual's failure to adopt the right attitudes in order to avoid poverty. It also suggests that those in poverty are not good at resolving problems and challenges, and not good at avoiding them in the first place.
In areas where the main industry has declined, such as mining regions in Yorkshire, there are few opportunities for work and getting out of poverty can be very difficult.	This model believes a culture has formed over generations which has bred a cycle of poverty. The poor need to break this cycle themselves by changing their attitudes.

Consequences of poverty

The consequences of poverty include:

- poor, damp, overcrowded housing
- lack of security
- poor health
- poor diet
- disease caused by poor housing (e.g. bronchitis, asthma and TB).

Poverty can affect a child's life chances and opportunities. If a child is more likely to suffer from ill health because they have poor health and poor housing conditions, then they are less likely to attend school lessons or extra curricular activities. This may mean they are less likely to progress well in education. Children receiving free school meals are half as likely to get five good GCSEs as those who are not. If they have fewer qualifications than others, it makes it more likely that they will then struggle to find employment as adults and will fall into the cycle of poverty.

Typical mistake

Students sometimes make the mistake of explaining why *they* think poverty exists in the UK. It is important to refer to different perspectives on poverty when answering a question on its possible causes. This is because the reasons for poverty in the UK are difficult to assess and so it has become a topic which is widely debated with many varying opinions on its definition, causes and cure.

Websites

Child Poverty Action Group is a charity campaigning for the abolition of child poverty: www.cpag.org.uk
Shelter is a housing and homeless charity: http://england.shelter.org.uk

Notions of underclass and poverty cycle

There are two models that we can refer to when looking at **underclass** and the poverty cycle and these are the structural model and the individual behaviour model:

> **Underclass** – a group in society who, over generations, are excluded from normal society because they are either unable to break the poverty cycle or are vulnerable and isolated or are criminal.

Perspective of structural model	Perspective of individual behaviour model
From this perspective, the poverty cycle is a trap that is beyond an individual's control.	From this perspective, the poverty cycle is a result of lifestyle choices and attitude.
For example, living in an area of high unemployment or growing up in a welfare-dependent household can effectively trap an individual into a cycle of poverty, meaning that they will be unlikely to have the skills or opportunity to find work.	Attitudes and behaviours such as poor attitude to education, a negative outlook on the future, disregard for authority and the law, sexual promiscuity and resulting unwanted pregnancies mean that individuals and communities do not remove themselves from poverty.
According to this model, an underclass is the product of society and only exists because certain communities have been neglected.	The poverty cycle is therefore self-constructed and can only be removed by those in poverty themselves.
The poverty cycle can only be broken if resources and support systems are available to help an individual lift themselves out of poverty.	In this model, the term 'underclass' means a group in society who are deeply entrenched in a culture of poverty characterised by unemployment and welfare dependency, with a disregard for law and a poor attitude to education. It is argued that this group is increasingly isolating itself from the normal values of society.

Examiner tip

When answering a question on poverty, where relevant ensure that your answer takes account of the many factors that may affect poverty, e.g. location, employment, disability, health, the cycle of poverty, opportunities and life chances.

Now test yourself

Tested

1 Why might it be difficult to define the term 'poverty'?
2 What is meant by the term 'underclass'?
3 Assess the causes of poverty in the UK.
4 Why do some argue that we should disregard the term 'poverty' in the UK?

Answers on pp.105–106

Exam practice

Examine some of the forms that discrimination may take.　**(10 marks)**

Answers and quick quiz online

Online

Examiner tip

This is a question that requires a short answer style response, asking you to discuss a range of forms of discrimination. The word 'some' implies that you do not have to cover every possible form of discrimination, but it also implies that several should be discussed.

A typical response may start with a broad definition of discrimination.

A range of forms would then be examined, for example: racial, age, sex, gender, disability and social class.

Chapter 4 How can discrimination and disadvantage be reduced?

4.1 What steps can government take to reduce discrimination and disadvantage?

The concept of equality in a changing and diverse society

Revised

Equality does not mean everyone being treated in exactly the same way. It means that, as far as possible, everyone should be treated fairly and have **equal opportunities**. In order to achieve this, sometimes people have to be treated differently depending on their circumstances, e.g. a person that has to use a wheelchair cannot be expected to use exactly the same facilities as someone that does not use a wheelchair.

As society becomes more diverse, the concept of equality increasingly involves celebrating and valuing difference, and striving to prevent discrimination on the grounds of gender, ethnicity, disability, social class, age and sexuality. **Legislation**, language, **policies** and media images have all changed in order to ensure that all groups in society are treated fairly.

Some people feel the expansion of **anti-discrimination policies** and law is a sign of political correctness gone too far, whereas others see it as a sign of a progressive society.

> **Equal opportunity** – the principle that all people have the same opportunities in life.
>
> **Legislation** – a law or set of laws suggested by a government and made official by a parliament.
>
> **Policies** – plans made by government or organisations to try to tackle certain issues. Policies may be made by parties wishing to be elected into government. If and when they are successful, government then tries to turn these policies into law.
>
> **Anti-discrimination policy** – laws and actions designed to challenge discrimination and prejudice. Can be part of a school policy, a council policy or a government policy.

Anti-discrimination policies

Revised

Anti-discrimination policies may be put in place by government organisations or non-governmental organisations to try to target discrimination. They can relate to gender, ethnicity, disability, sexual orientation, social class and age.

Local governments and schools may have anti-discrimination policies which attempt to interpret existing legislation and explain their approach to reducing or combating discrimination. These kinds of policies might include the following:

- promoting and protecting equality
- challenging discrimination
- raising awareness
- advising other organisations
- promoting positive role models.

> **Typical mistake**
>
> Only quote specific pieces of legislation if you are confident that you can remember their name and date. It is best not to attempt to guess or write part of the name or year. See page 30 for specific examples of anti-discrimination policies.

Dealing with direct and indirect discrimination

Revised

Direct discrimination	Indirect discrimination
This is a situation where someone is intentionally treated less favourably because of their gender, age, ethnicity, sexuality, disability, religion or belief.	This type of discrimination tends to be more subtle and may be unintentional.
This type of discrimination is rare in modern times as most employers and organisations are well aware of legislation on this issue and have ensured that their organisations comply with anti-discrimination legislation.	An example might be a job application that states applicants must be able to work until 8pm. This would indirectly discriminate against women as they are less likely to apply for this job as they tend to have primary childcare responsibility and so are probably less able to meet the job specification. In this instance women are being treated less favourably than men.
It is often easier to identify direct than indirect discrimination. Examples would include someone in a pub not serving someone because of their sexual orientation or an organisation that does not allow membership to someone because of their ethnicity.	Indirect discrimination may be harder to identify and prove. Any individual who feels they have been directly or indirectly discriminated against in the workplace can take their case to an Employment Tribunal.

Exemptions where discrimination is allowed/justified

Some exemptions exist to the Equality Act 2010, whereby employers are allowed to directly discriminate, these include:

- **Priests, monks, nuns, rabbis and ministers of religion**: as such individuals must adhere to a particular religion to do their job.

- **Actresses, actors and models in the film, television and fashion industries**: because certain roles require particular characteristics, e.g. male or female.

- **Employees working in an environment with cultural or gender sensitivities (e.g. a woman's clinic).**

- **Political parties who run all-female shortlists:** some political parties attempt to make their organisations more representative of wider society and so create a list of all-female candidates so the potential representative for that constituency can only be a woman.

Legislation relating to equal opportunities

Revised

Legislation	Details
Equal Pay Act 1970	Prohibits less favourable treatment of either men or women in terms of pay and conditions of employment. It entitles men and women to the same pay for doing the same jobs/work.
Sex Discrimination Act 1975	Protects men and women from discrimination on the grounds of their sex or because they are married. It concerns conditions of employment, training and education, the provision of goods or services, and issues of harassment.
Race Relations Act 1976	Was created to prevent discrimination on the grounds of race. It concerns discrimination on the grounds of race, colour, nationality, ethnic and national origin in relation to employment, the provision of goods and services and education.
Equality Act 2006	The areas the Act specifically deals with include age; disability; gender; proposed, commenced or completed gender reassignment; race; religion or belief and sexual orientation. It created the Equality and Human Rights Commission (EHRC).
Equality Act 2010	This Act effectively merged the many pieces of anti-discrimination legislation into one Act. The provisions of the Equal Pay Act 1970, Sex Discrimination Act 1975, Race Relations Act 1976 and the Disability Discrimination Act 1995 were all consolidated under this piece of legislation.

Policies relating to equal opportunities

New Deal	This was a policy of the Labour government in 1998. It was introduced to challenge discrimination and social disadvantage. It offered financial support and help to those citizens who were actively seeking employment, to help them find and keep a job. The 'deal' was that if you were actively looking for work, the government would help you to secure a job. It has since been replaced by a similar scheme by the coalition government called the Work Programme.
Minimum wage	This was also a policy of the Labour government. The minimum wage policy was introduced in 2009. Most workers are entitled to a national minimum level of pay. It offers different rates of pay to four different groups: ● 16–17-year-olds (workers above school leaving age but under 18) ● 18–20-year-olds ● an apprentice rate for apprentices under 19, or in the first year of their apprenticeship ● those aged 21 or over. The policy was introduced in an attempt to protect vulnerable groups in low income roles. It was opposed by employers who feared they would lose profits by paying higher wages and possibly jeopardise their businesses.

Government bodies created to develop equal opportunities

The Equality and Human Rights Commission (EHRC) was created by the Equality Act 2006. It merged several other existing bodies designed to prevent discrimination:

● Commission for Racial Equality

● Disability Rights Commission

● Equal Opportunities Commission.

The EHRC:

● promotes the interests of groups that may face hurdles to equal opportunities, and informs the public on these issues

● provides legal advice to companies on how to promote equal opportunities, and to employees who feel they have been unfairly treated

● publishes reports on specific areas of discrimination in order to highlight inequalities and also to inform legislation.

> **Websites**
>
> Directgov: Information on the current rates of the National Minimum Wage: www.direct.gov. uk/en/Employment/Employees/ TheNationalMinimumWage
> **The Equality and Human Rights Commission website:** www.equalityhumanrights.com

> **Examiner tip**
>
> Be sure to read questions carefully; if a question does not refer specifically to government but asks 'what can be done to reduce discrimination?' then it is advisable to respond by detailing the work of both governmental and non-governmental organisations.

> **Examiner tip**
>
> Exam questions on the topic of discrimination will often ask you to assess what government has done to reduce discrimination. It is useful to remember that government may refer to local government as well as central government.

Now test yourself

1 What is meant by 'equality' within the context of equal opportunities?

2 Why might indirect discrimination be harder to identify than direct discrimination?

3 Identify three policies or legislation created to combat discrimination and disadvantage and explain how they improve life chances.

4 Outline the role of the Equality and Human Rights Commission.

Answers on p.106

4.2 How effective have anti-discrimination policies been?

Strengths and weaknesses of current legislation

Revised

Unfortunately, some groups and individuals still become victims of discrimination and disadvantage even though governments have created policies and legislation to attempt to prevent it. This is mainly due to continued prejudice within society that in turn pervades companies, education and other organisations.

Strengths of current legislation	Weaknesses of current legislation
If an employer or public authority breaches current discrimination legislation they can be prosecuted. Compensation can be sought via tribunals or the court system.	Cases can be complex and establishing whether discrimination has occurred is often open to interpretation.
As some legislation has existed for over 30 years, there are now substantial case studies/histories that can be used to identify examples of discrimination.	Indirect discrimination sometimes occurs without the individual realising it.
Good guidance exists to give examples of how legislation should be applied.	Challenging discrimination can be daunting – especially if it concerns an employer as individuals may be worried about working relationships and costs.
Successful prosecution of discrimination can send a clear message to public authorities and employers that discrimination will not be tolerated.	Employers may be careful to hide their discrimination and assert various other reasons for an employee's treatment, i.e. redundancy as a cost-cutting measure rather than discrimination against individuals because of their sex, ethnicity, health issues or disability.
Over time, existing legislation changes attitudes and in turn impacts cultural and societal norms.	People's prejudices can be difficult to challenge regardless of whether legislation or policies exist to combat it.

Typical mistake

When answering a question on the effectiveness of anti-discrimination policies or legislation, students have stated that prejudice is 'unavoidable', 'impossible to change' or 'natural'; and that this means it is not worth challenging. There is validity in the points that prejudice may be:

a) widespread in some areas

b) common in relation to a particular group

c) possibly an unconscious psychological strategy that enables humans to simplify their surroundings in order to comprehend the wider world.

However, none of the above warrants the assertion that prejudice and discrimination should not be tackled.

The changing perception of equal opportunities in the UK

Revised

The ways in which society has developed and changed its perception of certain groups in order to ensure equal opportunities can be seen in stages.

Stage One ⟶	Stage Two ⟶	Stage Three
Political and legal rights championed	Legal rights are secured	Social and cultural equality
e.g. women campaigning for and then gaining the right to vote in order to participate politically.	e.g. women gaining the right to equal pay and the passing of anti-discrimination laws.	e.g. attitudes to women change and equal opportunities between men and women are expected by society.

Equal rights legislation has developed chronologically, gradually ensuring individuals are not discriminated on the basis of sex, race, disability, sexual orientation or age.

1970s and 1980s	Equal pay legislation adapted to include discrimination on grounds of sex. Legislation on racial discrimination was strengthened to ensure that provision was made to ensure public bodies were effective in preventing race discrimination.
1998	Legislation required organisations and public spaces had to ensure disabled access.
2000	The concept of institutional racism is developed from the Macpherson report into the police handling of the murder of teenager Stephen Lawrence after it declared the Metropolitan Police were routinely racist. This meant the force had to begin analysing their policies and practices to check they were not inherently racist. Other organisations had to do the same and broaden the process to ensure against discrimination on the grounds of sex, disability and age.
2006	The state recognises the legal status of same-sex marriages. Discrimination on grounds of age is no longer legal.

Now test yourself

Tested ☐

1 Outline two main strengths and weaknesses of existing anti-discrimination policies/legislation.

2 What are some of the problems affecting the success of anti-discrimination legislation or policies?

3 Briefly describe the process of how anti-discrimination legislation can change wider attitudes of society.

Answers on p.106

Examiner tip

When assessing the effectiveness of anti-discrimination policies and legislation, the examiner will be looking for analysis of both strengths and weaknesses so be sure to discuss both.

Exam practice

Examine the role of government over the past 50 years in tackling discrimination in the UK. **(15 marks)**

Answers and quick quiz online

Online ☐

Examiner tip

The focus of this question is on government policy regarding discrimination since the end of the Second World War, and the ways in which the government has intervened.

Here is a possible structure to your answer:

1 Define discrimination.

2 Describe briefly how the definition of discrimination and the groups involved have changed over the last 50 years, from equality for women to ageism.

3 Describe the role that the government has undertaken in tackling discrimination: passing laws, establishing regulation and regulatory bodies, developing policy initiatives and funding projects.

4 Briefly conclude with an overview regarding the success or not of the measures that were taken.

Chapter 5 What are rights?

5.1 Concept of a 'right' and the relationship between rights and duties

The fundamental nature of rights Revised

Rights are a pivotal aspect of any legal system. The existence of rights within a society means:

- there must be a legal system in place that recognises those rights
- the legal system can enforce those rights
- no one can stop a person from exercising their rights.

A legal system is defined by the following principles. It must:

- be binding on the whole of society
- reflect the moral attitudes of society
- evolve to reflect changing moral values
- punish people who commit criminal offences
- ensure contracts between people/companies are honoured.

Sometimes citizens may believe they have the 'right' to do certain things, however it is essential to understand that rights only exist in the presence of the rule of law. Citizens only have rights that are protected or permitted by law. For example, many people would assume that they have the right to buy an alcoholic drink in a pub if they are over the age of eighteen years. However, as the landlord of the pub can legally refuse entry to anyone under the Licensing Act 2003, and can legally refuse to serve an alcoholic drink to anyone, citizens do not actually have the right to buy an alcoholic drink in the pub as they need the permission of another person (the landlord) to do so.

> **Rights** – in this context, these are the privileges, liberties, powers and immunities that are recognised by a legal system.

Rights as building blocks in legal theory Revised

Rights, in a legal sense, come from specific **statutes**, laws made by Parliament. Statutes are the most common source of law but the European Union (via European legislation) and the court system (via precedent, where decisions made by courts are binding on lower courts) can also affect law, and therefore rights.

> **Statute** – a law made by Parliament (also known as an 'Act').

The table below shows examples of rights and the source of law that they come from.

Right	Source
Right to free education	Education Act 1944
Right to vote in an election for men and women over eighteen	Representation of the People Act 1969
Rights if arrested	Serious Organised Crime and Police Act 2005
Right to buy alcohol	Licensing Act 2003

Analysis of rights and duties

 Revised

Along with rights, the law also assumes duties. These duties might be between individuals or they might be duties that are assumed of the state or an organisation.

In the case of *Donoghue* V. *Stevenson*, 1932, May Donoghue suffered severe gastroenteritis after drinking ginger beer from a bottle that she later discovered contained a decomposed snail. She sued the manufacturer of the ginger beer, James Stevenson. When the case was eventually heard in the House of Lords, they decided that the manufacturer of the beer had a duty to avoid injuring persons who would purchase and consume his products without the opportunity of inspecting them. The leading judgement was made by Lord Atkin. He said 'You must take reasonable care to avoid acts or omissions which you can reasonably foresee would be likely to injure your neighbour.'

The term 'neighbour' here means anyone that you could reasonably foresee would be affected by the action. Duties, as well as rights, are therefore evident in our legal system.

Rights and duties as the basis for legal relationships

Revised

Rights and duties are pivotal to a justice system. The premise that each citizen's right has a corresponding duty is important in trying to resolve disputes between citizens, and disputes between citizens and the state, companies or organisations. Rights and duties set out what is expected of individuals or organisations in various settings. **Criminal law** and **civil law** refer to different areas of our justice system.

Criminal law – area of law that is concerned with the state bringing proceeding against an individual to punish them for a breach in the law.

Civil law – area of law that is concerned with disputes between an individual and another (including companies or organisations).

Different views of rights and duties

Revised

Some duties have a corresponding right and some don't.

Relative duties	Duties that have a corresponding right, e.g. the duty to pay a debt has a corresponding right for a person to be paid what is owed to them.
Absolute duties	Duties that do not have a corresponding right, e.g. the duty of a citizen not to break the law.

The term 'rights' can be confusing because it is used to describe many different types of rights, and the range of rights and duties are quite different from each other. See the table at the top of page 36.

Claim right	A right that infers a corresponding duty to the right-holder. This means that someone else must do or refrain from doing something to or for the claim holder. For example, the right to free education infers a duty from others to provide free education (in the case of the UK, this means the state).
Liberty right	A 'freedom' or permission to do something – there are no corresponding duties or obligations owed by anyone else to enable a liberty right. For example, freedom of speech can be enjoyed by citizens but others are not under any obligation to enable them to speak or listen to them.

Typical mistake

Avoid confusion with the topic of 'human rights' at this stage. A broad based question on rights, or rights and duties, might warrant *some* information and analysis on issues surrounding human rights. However, ensure that you read the question carefully and be sure to distinguish between rights and duties as the basis for legal relationships and any specific human rights legislation, e.g. Human Rights Act, 1998.

Examiner tip

Ensure you can identify why rights are important:

1 They enable citizens to do the things they need to without interference from the state.

2 They afford liberty within the rule of law to all citizens, equally.

3 They can include corresponding duties to ensure individuals or organisations take reasonable care of others.

4 They form the basis for dispute resolution.

Now test yourself   Tested ☐

1 Where do rights come from?

2 How can a legal system be defined?

3 Identify and give examples of two different types of duties.

4 What is the difference between a claim right and a liberty right?

Answers on p.106

5.2 Different types of rights

Practical examples of rights in society ————————————— Revised ☐

The table below gives some of the rights that we have in the UK and the legislation or laws from which they originate.

Right	Statute/legislation that enables that right
Right to vote	Representation of the People Act 1969
Right to free education or training until the age of eighteen	Education Act 1944 and subsequent Education Acts
Right to practise religion	Human Rights Act 1998
Right to a fair trial	Human Rights Act 1998

Determining the powers of citizens

It is difficult to define what a 'right' actually is. The meaning varies according to the context in which it is used. However, there is a broad agreement that a particular individual having a right means:

- there is a legal system in place
- under the rules of that legal system, some other person has an obligation to do something or to abstain from doing something
- this obligation is made law and depends on the choice of the particular individual – the individual can choose whether the other person has to do the act or abstain from doing the act.

This asserts that if a person has a right, there is a law which says in particular circumstances that particular individuals can require some other person either to do something or refrain from doing something.

As social, economic and political factors change in society, the law must also adapt in order to remain fair and relevant. This means rights and duties will change too. The term to describe this constantly changing aspect of law is 'dynamic'.

Often legal cases will highlight the need for a change or clarification in law that affects rights – an example of this is the *Donoghue* V. *Stevenson* case (see page 35). Before this case came to court the duty of care to 'avoid acts and omissions which you can reasonably foresee would be likely to injure your neighbour' had not been formally recognised. However, the interpretation of the law by the House of Lords meant that in the future citizens had the right not to be injured through a manufacturer's negligence.

Conflicting rights

The rights of citizens originate with the legal system but occasionally this legal system must be used to settle disputes between citizens whose rights appear to be in conflict. Two or more people may have a valid right but those rights may conflict with each other.

The rights of parents and children can sometimes conflict, along with the rights of the individual and the state. The tables below and on page 38 outlines some examples of conflicting rights.

Case	Whose rights are conflicting?	Details	Outcome
Gillick v. West Norfolk and Wisbech Area Health Authority	Mrs Victoria Gillick (the right to be informed) and the rights of girls under sixteen years of age (the right to privacy)	Mrs Victoria Gillick took a case against West Norfolk and Wisbech Area Health Authority in 1985 as it had told the GPs it employed they were allowed to prescribe the contraceptive pill to girls under the age of sixteen (if they were sufficiently mature and understood what was involved). Mrs Gillick was a mother of ten daughters and a strict Roman Catholic with religious objections to birth control. She was concerned that GPs would be able to prescribe the contraceptive pill without her knowledge.	Mrs Gillick brought an application to the High Court asking for a declaration that the Health Authority was wrong. She lost in the High Court but won in the Court of Appeal. The Health Authority then appealed to the House of Lords, whereby by a majority of three to two the House of Lords agreed that West Norfolk and Wisbech Area Health Authority was correct in its advice to GPs.

Case	Whose rights are conflicting?	Details	Outcome
Evans v. United Kingdom	Ms Natalie Evans (the right to a family life) and Mr Howard Johnston (the right to withdraw consent)	Natalie Evans was diagnosed with ovarian cancer in 2001 and as a result was offered IVF treatment as her fertility would be affected. Six embryos were created using Ms Evans' eggs and the sperm of Howard Johnston (her then fiancé). In 2002 the couple split up and Mr Johnston requested that the embryos be destroyed. UK law states that both parties must give consent for IVF to continue.	Ms Evans challenged the existing UK law as she claimed her rights under the European Convention of Human Rights had been breached. She took her case to the High Court but was unsuccessful. She then took her case to the European Court of Human Rights and was again unsuccessful. She finally lodged an appeal to the Grand Chamber of the European Court of Human Rights and they ruled against her. The embryos were destroyed.

Typical mistake

Students sometimes cite examples within their answers that, although valid, are not the best examples to ensure they achieve level 3 according to the mark scheme. Students should be aiming to 'demonstrate knowledge and understanding of specific citizenship issues' and then provide analysis of them. This is harder to do if the examples chosen do not allow lots of scope for specific analysis.

For instance, saying that 'the right to own a dog conflicts with someone else's right not to be disturbed by that dog's barking' would not be the best example of conflicting rights because it is difficult to analyse from which legislation these two rights originate.

Examiner tip

An exam question may ask you for examples of how citizens' rights conflict in relation to this area of the specification. Be sure to use examples that concern genuine rights, i.e. those rights originating in law. They might be rights originating from the Human Rights Act 1998 or from another piece of legislation.

Now test yourself

Tested ☐

1 Give a practical example of three rights and explain the statue/legislation from which they originate.
2 Why is the law described as 'dynamic'?
3 Detail an example of how citizens' rights may conflict.
4 How might citizens resolve conflicting rights?

Answers on pp.106–107

Exam practice

Assess the extent to which UK citizens have both rights and responsibilities. **(15 marks)**

Answers and quick quiz online

Online ☐

Examiner tip

The key to this short essay response question is to ensure that there is an equal balance between the points made regarding rights and those made about responsibilities. A possible route through this question is:

1 Briefly define the terms 'rights' and 'responsibilities'.
2 Develop a series of case studies where you can contrast the rights and responsibilities of UK citizens, e.g. human rights, legal rights and political rights.
3 Bring together your arguments about the balance between rights and responsibilities in regards to UK citizens.

Chapter 6 What rights do I have?

6.1 Human rights

The principles of human rights
Revised

In most democratic countries, the rights of citizens are held in a constitution (see page 9). If this is written down in a single document, it is known as a codified constitution. Codified constitutions are difficult to change.

However, the UK does not have a written constitution. The rights of citizens and the rules of government are all clearly known but some of them are written in statutes, some come from decisions made in the courts and some come from long-standing custom and practice. This is known as an uncodified constitution. There is no single document that sets out the rights of British citizens. Uncodified constitutions can be changed relatively easily because Parliament can change the law at any time. Parliament has **parliamentary sovereignty**.

As there is no written constitution enshrining rights in the UK, citizens are free to do anything that is not prohibited by law – this is a system of **residual freedoms**. This system can be seen as successful because it has been in place for around 300 years. However, as the citizen can do anything that is not illegal, the government can also interfere with the rights of citizens if there is not a law specifically prohibiting it.

> **Parliamentary sovereignty** – the principle that Parliament is the supreme law maker. This means that Parliament can make any law it wants to and it can change any law made in the past or by the interpretation of the courts.

The European Convention on Human Rights
Revised

What?	A treaty made by the countries who signed it, agreeing to give their citizens the basic rights contained within it.
When?	The treaty was signed in 1950 and ratified (into law) in 1951. It became binding in 1953.
Why?	The recognition that many of the horrors of the Second World War were inflicted on citizens because their human rights had not been protected. The Holocaust had seen the extermination of millions of people because they were Jewish, homosexual or disabled.
Who?	Originally created by the Council of Europe. Now 45 countries have signed the European Convention on Human Rights.
How?	Any citizen of a state that has signed the ECHR can take their case to the European Court of Human Rights in Strasbourg (a court created by the convention).

As it was an international agreement, the European Convention on Human Rights did not change the domestic law of the countries signed up to it (the signatories). This meant that if a UK citizen felt that their human rights had been breached, they had to go through the entire UK court system before a case could be heard in the European Court of Human Rights in Strasbourg. This was a long and expensive process.

Summary of rights contained in the European Convention on Human Rights

1   The right to life
2   Freedom from torture
3   Freedom from slavery or forced labour
4   The right to liberty and security
5   The right to a fair trial
6   The prohibition of retrospective criminal laws
7   The right to private life, family life, home and correspondence
8   The right to freedom of thought, conscience and religion
9   The right to freedom of expression
10 The right to freedom of peaceful assembly and association
11 The right to marry
12 The right to enjoy rights protected in ECHR without discrimination
13 The right to an education
14 The right to participate in elections
15 The right not to be subjected to death penalty

Protocol 1

Article 1. The right to peaceful enjoyment of private possessions

Article 2. The right not to be denied access to education system

Article 3. The right to free and fair elections by secret ballot

Protocol 4

The right to move freely within a state

> **Typical mistake**
>
> Students often confuse the European Convention on Human Rights with the European Courts of Justice, the court of the European Union. The ECHR is not connected in any way with the EU.

> **Typical mistake**
>
> Students may make the mistake of confusing issues of criminal law and human rights. For example, when asked to cite an example of how a human right can be breached, students have discussed murder of an individual by another citizen as an example of a breach of the right to life. The intentional taking of an individual's life by another is a criminal offence – murder. The ECHR and HRA deal with the rights an individual has in relation to the state, not other individuals.

The Human Rights Act 1998   Revised ☐

What?	The Human Rights Act (HRA) is an Act of Parliament which incorporated the ECHR into UK law.
When?	The HRA came into force in the UK on 2 October 2000.
Why?	Although the ECHR existed, it was difficult for citizens to seek redress if they felt their rights under the convention had been abused. The HRA meant that the ECHR was now part of UK law and so judges in the UK could apply the convention.
Who?	The HRA was a piece of legislation created by Tony Blair's Labour Government.
How?	A UK citizen can use the HRA to seek redress for a breach of their human rights, as stated in the European Convention, by taking their case to any British court.

The Human Rights Act 1998 made the following changes:

● Made it easier for a UK citizen to seek redress for abuse of their Convention rights via any British court.

● UK courts must interpret all legislation in a way that is compatible with the ECHR.

● Government or any public authority cannot behave in a way that is not compatible with the ECHR.

● The government must publish a statement as to whether or not any new bill introduced is compatible with the ECHR.

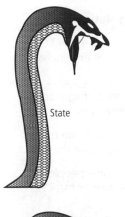

State

Citizen

Rights

Figure 1.2

The contemporary debate about the impact of human rights legislation

Revised

There has been increasing debate surrounding the human rights legislation in the UK. The following case studies have been cited as examples where the Human Rights Act is either working in the spirit in which it was created, or where it is affording rights to those that do not 'deserve' them.

Case Study	Details
Abu Qatada	Abu Qatada is a Muslim refugee to the UK, granted leave to remain in 1994. It was claimed that he had links to al-Qaeda (the terrorist group that was responsible for the attacks on the United States on 11 September 2001) and that he preached sermons justifying the killing of non-Muslims. He was imprisoned in the UK under anti-terrorism legislation but later placed under a form of house arrest after the Law Lords ruled that his imprisonment was illegal. He was then released under very strict bail conditions. He started a legal case against the UK because he was threatened with deportation to Jordan where he faced other charges. He argued that evidence obtained through his previous torture in Jordan would be used against him there. The European Court of Human Rights ruled that he should not be deported to face trial in Jordan.
Beryll and Richard Driscoll	Beryll and Richard Driscoll got married in 1940. In later life, Mr Driscoll became ill and had to go to live in a care home. His wife wanted to live in the care home with him as they had not lived apart in the 65 years they had been married (except during Mr Driscoll's war service in Burma). Gloucestershire social services would not allow her to do this as they said she was able to look after herself, even though she was registered blind. Using the Human Rights Act they managed to persuade the council to reverse its decision and offer Mrs Driscoll a subsidised place in the same care home as her husband.

Arguments for human rights legislation	Arguments against human rights legislation
Rights of UK citizens have been strengthened by the HRA.	Citizens enjoyed rights in many countries before the ECHR was created and the Human Rights Act is not entrenched and could be repealed at any time.
Even if the HRA were repealed by Parliament, the UK is still a signatory of the ECHR.	Countries are still allowed to stray from their obligations to carry out most of the rights in times of emergency.
The HRA avoids conflict between domestic and international law.	HRA gives too much power to judges that must interpret it, possibly causing conflict between Parliament and the courts.
Gives rights to all humans equally.	The HRA should not apply to all because some people in society should not be entitled to all of their rights, i.e. convicted criminals.
The wrongdoer can be made to pay compensation in cases of human rights violation.	
It is now cheaper for a citizen to seek a remedy for a violation of rights under the Human Rights Act.	The ECHR is not drafted in the same way as UK statute. European legislation is drafted in wider terms, whereas UK statute tends to be more detailed. This leads to variations in how it is interpreted in different European countries.
It is more convenient and less time-consuming to seek redress for human rights breaches in the UK as the HRA means a citizen can take a case to any British court. Previously it took around six years to take a case to the European Court of Human Rights.	

There is currently a debate surrounding Human Rights legislation in the UK. In its 2010 General Election Manifesto, The Conservative Party pledged to introduce a 'British Bill of Rights' to replace the HRA 1988. After the 2010 General Election, the Conservatives formed a coalition government with the Liberal Democrats who oppose such a change. It has been agreed that there will be a commission set up to study the issue.

Now test yourself

Tested

1 Explain the terms 'constitution' and 'parliamentary sovereignty'.
2 Which events led to the European Convention on Human Rights being instigated?
3 Why did some feel the Human Rights Act 1998 was necessary, even though the ECHR was in existence?
4 What are the arguments against the creation of the HRA?

Answers on p.107

6.2 The right to know

The 'right to know' is inextricably linked to the 'right to freedom of expression'. As well as the right to make a point and influence opinion, this concerns an individual's right to **scrutinise** and challenge the government.

> **Scrutiny** – careful and detailed examination of something in order to establish its facts.

Through scrutiny, citizens can ensure government is acting lawfully and in the best interests of the citizens. This is key to a healthy democracy. If they cannot scrutinise government, they cannot make a decision about whether or not they want to vote for that government in elections, or consider how to vote in referendums.

Additionally, if individuals can check the information held by the government about them, it can protect citizens' rights from abuse by the state.

The **Data Protection Act (DPA) 1998** concerns personal information held by government about individuals. The **Freedom of Information Act (FOIA) 2010** concerns official documents and documents held by organisations which may have a public interest.

Exam practice answers and quick quizzes at **www.therevisionbutton.co.uk/myrevisionnotes**

The Data Protection Act (DPA) 1998 — Revised

What were the aims of the DPA?	• To protect the information held on an individual. • To allow access to a person's information if they request it.
What are the implications?	Any organisation has a responsibility to keep records held on an individual safely. The loss or misuse of personal data can lead to prosecution under law. All organisations such as businesses, schools and hospitals must allow the public free access to the information that an organisation has on them. Requests must be in writing, and then responded to within 40 days, except schools who must respond within fifteen working days. Organisations must also ensure that they keep citizens' information safe, which is increasingly important as identity theft has become more common.
Why might you request information held about you?	You might request the information held about you by your doctor in order to check that it is correct. You may also want to check the information held about you by a credit card company on your credit history. You may simply be interested to see what an organisation knows about you. The Information Commissioner's Office was established to provide information on citizen's rights in relation to information and handle complaints by citizens with regards to the DPA and FOIA (see below).
Exemptions	It would not be possible to request information held about another individual as this would be a breach of the DPA itself.
Case Study	Hertfordshire County Council was fined £100,000 by the Information Commissioner after employees accidentally sent two faxes containing details of a child sex abuse case, domestic violence records and care proceedings for three children to the wrong recipients on two separate occasions.

The Freedom of Information Act (FOIA) 2000 — Revised

What were the aims of the FOIA?	• To ensure that citizens can ask public authorities if they hold any information on a particular subject. It aimed to achieve more **transparency** in terms of government activities.
Implications	If a public body fails to respond to a request, release information or gives an inappropriate reason for not responding then a citizen can contact the Information Commissioner and ask them to investigate the decision. The term 'public body' is wide ranging. Examples are: central government, local government, the police, Further Education colleges and the National Health Service.
Why and how might you wish to request information	Anyone can apply for information without a particular reason for doing so. It may be that a citizen wants to ensure transparency regarding a particular government decision or actions. • The application must be made to the relevant department in writing. • It may cost a fee. • The authority may request more information in order to clarify the request. • The authority must respond within twenty days. Any information revealed via an FOI request is not confidential, so may then be published in other formats.
Exemptions	Under the FOIA there are several reasons a public authority can give for not supplying information requested. These mainly fall under the following: • The information is too sensitive in terms of national security or relations with other countries. • The request is unnecessary as the information will be, or is, already published. • The request would cost too many man hours or too much money to supply the information. • The request is vexatious (has been made before or is being made to waste time). • The information requested is legally privileged, for example communications between the Queen and the government are confidential. • The request concerns personal information or commercial confidences. If a citizen is unhappy with the way their FOI request has been dealt with or the time it has taken to respond (in excess of twenty working days) then they can ask the public authority concerned to launch an internal review of the way the request has been dealt with. If they are still unsatisfied, they can complain to the Information Commissioner's Office who can then investigate.
Case Study	Figures released as a result of Freedom of Information requests revealed that at least 944 currently serving police officers and police community support officers (PCSOs) have a criminal record.

Transparency – a situation whereby activities are done in an open way without secrets. This is to ensure fairness and honesty.

The contemporary debate about the FOIA

Revised

Advantages of the Freedom of Information Act	Criticisms of the Freedom of Information Act
Citizens have relatively easy access to information that may have previously been 'hidden' by government. This allows for more open government.	There are instances in which government has been accused of exploiting the exemptions in the FOI in order to avoid disclosing information.
Journalists have increasingly used FOI requests to uncover government mistakes or wrongdoing, increasing the scope of freedom of the press.	Many individual FOI requests can take up a large volume of civil servants' time and therefore cost government departments and public bodies an increasing amount of money.
It allows greater transparency on how government decisions are made, thus enabling greater checks on government actions to ensure they are just and lawful.	Trivial or malicious FOI requests submitted by individuals can waste time and money for very little benefit to the public interest.
Although the Freedom of Information Act has been criticised for costing government departments too much money, this spending is relatively low when compared to other departmental costs.	Money spent on responding to FOI requests could be better spent on public services.

Typical mistake

Ensure that you do not confuse the aims and procedures in regards to the FOI and DPA. Be clear in your responses that the 'right to know' concerns the right of the individual citizen to know information held by the government.

It doesn't concern the information held by individuals about each other.

Examiner tip

Exam questions may ask candidates about 'the right to know' rather than referring specifically to the Freedom of Information or Data Protection Acts, however you must ensure that you mention both in order to achieve maximum marks.

Now test yourself

Tested

1 What was the aim of the Data Protection Act?
2 What was the aim of the Freedom of Information Act?
3 How are freedom of expression and the right to know linked?
4 Why might information be withheld by a public authority?

Answers on p.107

6.3 Other rights of UK citizens

Rights not protected by the Human Rights Act

Revised

UK citizens enjoy a range of rights that are not protected by the human rights legislation that has been passed into law. Theoretically, citizens have the right to do anything they wish, as long as it is not illegal. However, it may be difficult for citizens to defend a right if it is not specifically protected by law. There is also some ambiguity in relation to whether 'rights' not protected by the Human Rights Act are in fact 'rights' at all.

Welfare rights

Details	Issues
Health: In the UK, the NHS provides healthcare that is free at the point of use. This means it is paid for via taxation so that users do not have to pay every time they use it.	The rights within the ECHR are mainly political. This is because it is difficult to find a consensus among the countries that have signed the European Convention on Human Rights as to what constitutes a basic requirement in terms of social and economic rights.
Education: Free education is provided to all in the UK until the age of sixteen (this will change to eighteen in 2015). Subsidies also exist for many adults who wish to remain in education. This is to enable all citizens to access education.	Different countries may also have ideological conflicts surrounding how much a government should be expected to provide for its citizens.
Housing: The state has made provisions to fund housing for UK citizens who find themselves without a home.	The provision for welfare rights is created by various complex statues and delegated legislation. There is nothing within the ECHR, and therefore nothing within the HRA, that protects these rights.
Disability: If a citizen is disabled and therefore unable to work, an allowance is paid to them by the government.	Although the HRA protects the right to access education, it does not prevent the UK government from introducing a charge for education. However, it is important to note that any government that did charge for education, or abolish the main provisions of the welfare state, would be likely to be so unpopular that it would be voted out of power at the next general election.
The elderly: When citizens reach 65 years of age they are able to claim a state funded pension. This will rise to 66 years of age between 2018 and 2020 and will rise to 68 years for those born after 1977.	
Unemployment: Any UK citizen that is out of work can claim unemployment benefit, although certain conditions may have to be met before they can receive it.	

Right to defend oneself

Details	Issues
There is a legal defence that can be claimed if a defendant is charged with assault and argues that they used necessary and reasonable force to protect themselves against an attack by the victim. There is no existing 'right' to defend oneself in the ECHR.	There is a 'right to a fair trial' contained in the HRA. Should a defendant not be allowed to claim the legal defence of self-defence then it could be argued that they had been denied a fair trial.
This defence allows a person to kill another if they do so in the act of defending themselves, but only if they can prove that they used necessary and reasonable force in doing so in order to defend their own life.	The ECHR was drafted in a general sense rather than laying out detailed specifics so it is difficult to assess to what extent the term 'fair' trial should be taken. The range of interpretation is so large that, for example, it could be taken to mean that all procedures within court should be fair and/or that laws themselves should be fair (e.g. in that they don't discriminate against anyone).
Tony Martin, a farmer, was convicted of murder after shooting dead one man and injuring another man who was burgling his home. This was because the jury found that Martin did intend to kill or cause serious bodily harm, rather than killing out of self-defence.	

Right to trial by jury

Details	Issues
Juries are usually found in criminal cases. They do not decide the sentence (that is the role of the judge) but they decide if the accused is guilty or not guilty. Juries can be used in some civil cases, but this is rare. The Human Rights Act does not specifically protect the right to trial by jury.	Although the HRA does protect the right to a fair trial it does not specifically protect the right to trial by jury.
	Only 1% (or approx. 30,000) criminal cases are tried by juries – the most serious cases. This means that in most cases citizens do not have a jury present to decide on whether they are guilty or not guilty. This should not be a problem as long as the other methods of hearing cases are fair (e.g. Magistrates' Courts). However, many people feel that trial by jury is the *fairest* way to hear a case.
	It is also worth noting that the process of using juries for trials is expensive and time consuming. This means that logistically their wider use is restricted.

Now test yourself

Tested ☐

1 From where do welfare rights derive in the UK?

2 Why is it unlikely that a government would abolish the welfare state in the UK?

3 Why is the right to defend oneself not contained in the Human Rights Act?

4 Why is the right to trial by jury not contained in the Human Rights Act?

Answers on p.107

Exam practice

Why do many people in the UK want to replace the Human Rights Act 1998 with a new Bill of British Rights? **(15 marks)**

Answers and quick quiz online

Online ☐

Examiner tip

This short essay-style response requires you to show understanding of the views of those who wish to replace the existing HRA 1998 with a British Bill of Rights. A possible route through this question:

1 Write a short statement about how the existing HRA is based upon the ECHR.

2 Why do some people want a change, and who are they? Changing the existing HRA is part of the policy of the Conservative Party which believes that the existing HRA gives limited discretion to national governments. They are also concerned about the workings of the Court in Strasbourg.

3 Describe case studies that support the case for change. (Remember *not* to confuse the Council of Europe and its work with that of the European Union.)

4 Conclude with comments about the potential for change – limited currently due to the coalition government and the Liberal Democrats' support for the HRA.

Chapter 7 The legal framework: protecting the citizen

7.1 Civil and criminal law

Criminal law and punishment
Revised

- The laws of a country are based on **morality**, widely held beliefs about what is right and wrong, what behaviour is acceptable and what is forbidden. In Western swocieties this is usually based on Christian views of morality.

- Not all forms of wrongdoing will be punished by law, but those that society believes are the most serious are punished.

- The main purpose of criminal law is to regulate and control society by punishing behaviour that society regards as seriously wrong or unacceptable.

- Laws change over time as general opinion changes about what is and is not acceptable. For example, it was once illegal in the UK for a woman to have an abortion, or for same-sex couples to have a sexual relationship.

- The state takes the defendant to court on behalf of the people. The case is heard as 'Regina verses *surname of defendant*'. Regina is the Latin term meaning 'Queen'.

- Examples of criminal law cases: theft, murder or assault.

- The police are usually called in to investigate crimes. The information and evidence that they collect is passed to the Crown Prosecution Service (CPS). CPS decides whether to prosecute suspects based on whether there is enough evidence to secure a conviction.

- Cases are heard in Magistrates' Court or Crown Court and a verdict of guilty or not guilty is made. After a person has been convicted, they are sentenced to a punishment, e.g. a fine, imprisonment or a community sentence such as a curfew or community service.

> **Morality** – a set of standards for behaviour, the guidelines for a belief about what is right and wrong.

> **Websites**
>
> HM Courts and Tribunals Service brings together HM Courts Service and Tribunals Service. As an agency of the Ministry of Justice it is responsible for the administration of the criminal, civil and family courts and tribunals in England and Wales:
> www.justice.gov.uk/about/hmcts

Civil law and compensation
Revised

- Civil law is concerned with the citizen seeking a remedy through the courts if they are in dispute with another individual or company/organisation. Civil courts offer a decision as to whether the claim of the 'claimant' is valid and can award compensation from one individual/company to another.

- Civil law is concerned with disputes between:
  - individuals and other individuals, or
  - individuals and companies, or
  - individuals and government departments.

- Cases can be heard in:
  - Small Claims Court (if claim for compensation is £5000 or less),
  - County Court (if claim for compensation is over £5000)
  - the High Court (if claim for compensation exceeds £50,000 or if the case concerns a difficult point of law or an issue that warrants High Court e.g. **defamation** or complaint about police).
- Civil courts may deal with a number of different types of case including:
  - **Divorce cases**: Civil courts divide couples' assets or decide on custody arrangements for children, because they cannot make the decision themselves.
  - **Terms of contracts**: courts can make a judgement about whether '**parties**' have followed the agreement laid out in a contract.
  - **Ownership of land**: civil courts may be asked to make a judgement on who owns a piece of land or property.
  - **Probate of wills**: civil courts may have to make decisions about whether a deceased person's will has been made correctly and on how their assets are distributed.

> **Defamation** – to damage the reputation of a person or group by saying or writing things about them which are not true.

> **Typical mistake**
>
> Ensure that you are clear that criminal courts do not award compensation – this is the role of civil courts – and conversely, civil courts do not hand down prison sentences to citizens.

> **Party** – one of the people or groups of people involved in an official argument or arrangement.
>
> **Probate** – the legal administration of a deceased person's will.

How the law enables citizens to make appropriate arrangements

Revised

An important function of civil law is to allow people to make contracts or arrangements that can be enforced – agreements that both parties know they will keep to or carry out.

Contracts: These may not always be written, for example when someone buys or sells something, there is an unwritten contract between them about what can be expected of the product and how much is to be paid for it. However, many contracts are written to prevent any confusion about the terms, and also to avoid any arguments about what is involved in the contract. Being able to make contracts and have confidence that they will be fulfilled is vital to society. Civil law plays a valuable role in ensuring that if the terms of an agreement or contract are not met, then an individual can take action to seek a remedy.

Wills: There are laws about how to distribute a person's **assets** after their death but an individual can make a will which bypasses the laws to distribute their property as they wish. The civil courts are often asked to make decisions about whether a will is valid or they may wish to dispute the legality or fairness of something in it.

> **Examiner tip**
>
> Ensure that you understand the differing nature of criminal law and civil law in terms of how their purposes and administration differ as well as the different types of cases they hear. Ensure you are also clear about the distinction between compensation and punishment.

> **Assets** – something valuable that belongs to a person. For example, their house.

Now test yourself

Tested

1 What is the purpose of both criminal law and civil law?
2 Explain the difference between the decisions a criminal court and civil court make.
3 Outline two other key differences between civil law and criminal law.
4 Why is it important that citizens can make use of the civil courts to settle disputes about contracts or wills?

Answers on p.107

7.2 Legal representation

The legal professions: solicitors and barristers

Revised

Solicitors and barristers both have similar roles. They:

- advise clients about the law and their rights
- draft legal documents
- represent clients in court.

However, there are also key differences in their work. The table below highlights each occupation and draws some comparisons.

Solicitors	Barristers	Analysis
• Nearly 100,000 solicitors in Britain. • Regulated by the Solicitors Regulation Authority which tries to ensure that the needs of the solicitor's client are met. • The Law Society has a trade association which looks after solicitors' interests. • Mainly office-based work involving **conveyancing,** drawing up wills and contracts, and giving oral and written advice to clients. • Solicitors usually represent their clients in Magistrates' Courts (where most cases are heard) or County Court. • Most solicitors work in partnership with other solicitors in 'firms' of solicitors.	• Only about 11,500 barristers in Britain. • Profession is collectively known as 'the Bar'. Their governing body is the Bar Council. • Barristers must remain self-employed and are not allowed to form partnerships. They usually share offices called 'chambers' so they can share administrative costs. • Barristers spend most of their time in court or preparing for court. They work mainly in higher courts (Crown Court and above). • Usually clients do not directly approach a barrister, they employ a solicitor who then engages a barrister if it is necessary. • They operate under the 'cab rank rule' which means that barristers must accept a case if it is in an area of their specialism, the fee is in line with their experience and they have no other commitments that will interfere.	**Similarities** • Training is broadly similar. • Both are practising **lawyers**. • Both do the same sort of work but in different ways. • Both are subject to strict professional rules. **Differences** • They have different ways of working; a barrister is self-employed and solicitors work in firms. • Solicitors can sue clients to recoup their fees but barristers cannot.

Conveyancing – the legal process of buying and selling a house.

Lawyers – a general term to describe a person skilled in the law.

- The Bar is needed by small firms of solicitors as they require access to specialist services for their clients, and only the largest firms of solicitors can facilitate this.
- Cab rank rule guarantees independent representation for all, regardless of how unpopular they are or their case is.
- Many argue that it could be cheaper for us to have a single legal profession rather than two separate professions, but having two allows for specialised advocacy.

Examiner tip

In the exam you may get a question about the differences between solicitors and barristers but it may also pose a longer question requiring you to analyse the two professions, e.g. looking at whether the two professions are both required or whether one is of more use than the other.

Funding civil disputes: the Legal Services Commission

An important part of the principle of a 'fair trial' is to provide financial assistance to those who cannot afford the cost of legal fees. This is especially important in civil cases where the losing party has to pay the winning party's fees along with their own. For this reason, the government can help citizens with the costs of legal fees or advice, sometimes known as 'legal aid'. The Legal Services Commission administers this 'legal aid'. It oversees the Community Legal Service and The Criminal Defence Service (see below).

Typical mistake

Students often fail to refer to relevant pieces of legislation, or misquote them. A useful piece of legislation to remember for this topic is the **Access to Justice Act 1999** as this legislation has helped to give solicitors the same rights as barristers to represent their clients in court but they have to complete additional training – they are then called solicitor advocates. It also means a barrister has to accept work directly from the public. This piece of legislation has also changed the system of providing financial help to those who needed legal advice, setting up the Community Legal Service and the Criminal Defence Service.

Community Legal Service	This is concerned with civil, not criminal, matters. It manages the Community Legal Service Fund which has a set amount of money designated by the Ministry of Justice each year. **This fund can be accessed by those who need to defend a civil action (defendant) and those who want to bring a civil action (claimant).** The type of help it funds may be advice and assistance, legal representation or help at court.
	It does not cover cases involving defamation, disputes around companies, partnerships, trusts, boundaries or personal injuries. Someone may also be refused funds because it has run out for that service for the year.
	Applicants for financial aid are **means tested**; their disposable income and disposable capital are both looked at to ascertain whether they can afford legal fees themselves. If their disposable income falls below the minimum level they will receive free help from the Community Legal Service. If it exceeds the maximum level they will not receive help. If it falls in between, they will receive help but will have to make a contribution towards it.
	Some services are also **merits tested** based on whether the case is important enough to warrant spending public money and whether there is a reasonable chance that it will be successful.

The Criminal Defence Service	This is concerned with criminal, not civil, cases. Funding is provided by demand rather than being a fixed amount. It would be unfair to deny funding to someone facing criminal charges who is unable to afford legal fees because they may face imprisonment – this would breach the principle of a fair trial.
	The Criminal Defence Service funds the duty solicitor scheme, direct funding to approved practitioners and public defenders.
Duty solicitor schemes	Duty solicitor firms operate in police stations and in Magistrates' Courts. Approved local solicitors use a rota system to provide services to those charged with criminal offences. In police stations this is to ensure each person has access to free, independent legal advice in private and to assist them during the interview process with police.
	In Magistrates' Courts, solicitors use a rota system to ensure that a solicitor is available to provide assistance or representation. This allows individuals free and independent advice or representation in court, ensuring the court proceedings are as fair as possible.
Directly funded schemes	The state can pay firms of solicitors to offer assistance to those charged with criminal offences. This includes advice and assistance, advocacy assistance (preparing a case and possibly representing them) or representation (possibly covering the cost of employing a barrister to represent in Crown Court and any appeal). Magistrates make the decision on whether to grant funding based on whether it is in the 'interests of justice'. This is based on whether the accused is likely to be imprisoned if found guilty, if there are important points of law involved or if the accused cannot understand the case against them because of language barriers or mental health issues.
Public defenders	The Legal Services Commission employs the Public Defender Service to provide independent advice, assistance and representation on criminal matters. Public Defenders may give people advice in custody or represent them in Magistrates' Courts or higher courts.

Other sources of advice and representation

- **Conditional fee agreements:** an agreement made between a solicitor and client that they will take no fee, or reduce their fee, if they lose the case but if they win the case they will take their usual fee plus an agreed additional percentage. However, the loser in the civil action will still have to pay the winners' legal costs, even if they are using a conditional fee agreement.
- **Community Legal Service Direct:** national telephone and website service available 24 hours a day, 7 days a week. Mainly concerned with social security benefits, housing and debt.
- **Criminal Defence Service Direct:** provides telephone advice to those detained by police for offences that will not result in imprisonment.
- **Law centres:** these receive money from central and local government and large law firms. They offer free, non-means tested advice and are mainly concerned with housing, immigration and employment.
- **Citizens Advice Bureaux:** funded by central government and easily accessible, they are mainly used by citizens with problems resulting from debt.

> **Websites**
>
> Citizens Advice Bureaux deliver advice on a number of issues including legal disputes, advice and help with finding representation or funding: www.citizensadvice.org.uk

Now test yourself

1 What are the key differences between barristers and solicitors?
2 What are the advantages of having two legal professions?
3 Why is it important that citizens are provided assistance with legal costs and why might it be more important in criminal cases?

Answers on pp.107–108

7.3 Alternative methods of resolving disputes

Negotiation, mediation, conciliation and arbitration

Rather than going through a civil court procedure, there are several alternative forms of dispute resolution (ADR) that can be used for civil cases. They can be used as a way to avoid:

- the expense of legal procedures (litigation)
- the stress that is involved in court cases
- the confrontational nature of court (this may sour relations between parties in the future)
- discussion of the details of the case in public
- the time-consuming nature of civil action through the courts system
- the inconvenience of court dates
- decisions made by judges that do not entirely satisfy either party.

Type of alternative dispute resolution	Details	Advantages	Disadvantages
Negotiation	Parties involved discuss issues and compromise or make a decision about how the issues can be resolved.	<ul><li>Very informal</li><li>No cost</li><li>Private.</li></ul>	The parties involved may not be able to make a decision or compromise.
Mediation	Parties discuss disputes with a neutral third party known as a mediator. The mediator does not disclose their own opinion but instead acts as a facilitator who helps the parties reach their own agreement.	<ul><li>Much cheaper than courts.</li><li>Parties reach their own agreement, it is therefore likely to be more effective than settlements that are forced on them.</li></ul>	<ul><li>The process may not lead to a settlement.</li><li>The process is not legally binding.</li></ul>
Conciliation	A conciliator is used to help to resolve a dispute but plays a more active role than a mediator, e.g. they might suggest grounds for a possible compromise.	<ul><li>Much cheaper than litigation.</li><li>It is entirely private.</li><li>Good success rate.</li></ul>	<ul><li>Process may not lead to a settlement and so parties may have to litigate anyway.</li><li>Can put pressure on claimants to settle in employment cases and mean that they might accept a lesser settlement than a tribunal would award.</li></ul>
Arbitration	Arbitration is the process where parties agree to have their dispute heard by a private arbitrator who will make a binding decision. Many commercial contracts contain clauses which say the parties will use arbitration to settle any disputes.	<ul><li>Can be cheaper than courts.</li><li>Decisions are binding and can be enforced by courts.</li><li>Parties can choose their own arbitrator.</li><li>Quicker than court proceedings.</li></ul>	<ul><li>No state funding for arbitration.</li><li>Professional arbitrators' fees can be high, so may be as expensive as courts.</li><li>Using professional arbitrators and lawyers might cause delays similar to those experienced in the court system.</li></ul>

Ombudsmen and tribunals

Revised

Other parts of the legal system include ombudsmen and tribunals.

	Details	Advantages	Disadvantages
Ombudsmen E.g. Financial Ombudsmen, Parliamentary and Health Service Ombudsmen	An ombudsman is an official who is appointed to check on government activity on behalf of an individual citizen and to investigate complaints that are made. This can be in a range of areas, e.g. health service, local government, legal services and housing.	<ul><li>The problem may be solved.</li><li>Can lead to recommended changes made to government agencies or public bodies.</li></ul>	<ul><li>Their powers are constrained by the fact that they cannot deal with matters that could be dealt with by courts.</li><li>Complaints must be made through an elected representative and so this can be a barrier to citizens wishing to scrutinise government actions.</li></ul>
Tribunals E.g. Employment Tribunal, Immigration and Asylum Tribunal	Tribunals are inferior courts. They deal with a large number of cases each year. A variety of subjects are dealt with by specialised tribunals. These include employment, health and social care, pensions, finance and commerce.	<ul><li>Can deal with specialised issues.</li><li>Simple and informal procedure.</li><li>Can be cheaper than conventional courts.</li><li>Can be quicker than the court system.</li></ul>	<ul><li>Applicants that pay legal professionals to represent them tend to be more successful which possibly highlights inequality for those that cannot afford this option.</li><li>Reasons for decisions reached are not always clear.</li></ul>

N.B. Tribunals are recognised as courts and so cannot be described as an 'alternative form of dispute resolution' (or ADR). This term refers usually to negotiation, mediation, conciliation and arbitration.

Examiner tip

An exam question on the advantages and disadvantages of alternative forms of dispute resolution is likely to be a 15 mark question. You have roughly one minute per mark on all of the questions and so will need to spend about 15 minutes writing your answer. It might be difficult to write about each form of ADR in detail in that time, so it is advisable to write about only three.

Typical mistake

Students sometimes make the mistake of writing down any knowledge they have on a subject, whether or not it is actually relevant to the question asked. For example, when asked about how courts protect the rights of citizens, some students have written at length about the details of ADR because that was all they could remember about courts. Although you may pick up marks for understanding that citizens can use alternatives to the court system like mediation and arbitration to protect their privacy, and therefore protecting an element of their rights, it is unlikely you will achieve the upper end of a level 2 or level 3 in the mark scheme.

Now test yourself

Tested ☐

1. Why might ADR be preferable to using the court system?
2. Distinguish between the processes of mediation, conciliation and arbitration.
3. Identify three situations which would be likely to result in the use of tribunals.
4. What is the function of ombudsmen?

Answers on p.108

Exam practice

Student protests 2010

Thousands of students demonstrated in towns and cities around the UK against the introduction of changes to university tuition fees and other educational cuts. Many of the students were under eighteen years old. In some cases, there were breeches in criminal law, as some protesters vandalised buildings and threw items at the police. Police then had to react to this law-breaking. It was a difficult balance for the police, as most of the students did not break the law and had every right to protest peacefully.

Your answers should refer to the passage as appropriate, but you should also include other relevant information.

Briefly explain the term 'criminal law'. **(5 marks)**

Answers and quick quiz online

Online ☐

Examiner tip

This question requires a short response. It relates to a source question. Your response should be concise and to the point. Support any definition with examples to show your understanding. You should be writing no more than four or five sentences.

Chapter 8 How do the courts protect my rights?

8.1 The role of the courts

The need to balance conflicting interests
Revised

Parliament creates laws in the form of statutes. However, those statues cannot detail exactly how the legislation should be applied in every instance. Therefore, it is the role of the courts to interpret legislation when specific cases are brought before them.

When new laws come into force, or there has been an amendment to existing laws, this could give rise to conflict of interests. Courts must balance the conflicting interests within a case in order to reach a judgement.

Roscoe Pound, an American legal academic, defined the types of interest into the following categories.

Individual interests	Social interests
The rights of individual citizens, e.g. in owning property, making contracts and having personal privacy.	Protecting the security of the state and its institutions, conserving resources and promoting public morality.

Pound argued that an interest could only be properly balanced against another interest if it was in the same category; individual and individual or social and social. If an individual interest is being pitted against a social interest, in most cases the social interest must take precedence.

The judicial process
Revised

Civil law and criminal law have different purposes but they function in similar ways. They reach decisions by applying the law to the facts that are proved.

A significant amount of our law comes from the decisions that courts have made themselves. The decisions made by higher courts are usually binding in lower courts; the higher courts set the precedent. This is known as the rules of *stare decisis*, which means 'let the decision stand' in Latin.

The hierarchy of the court system is as follows:

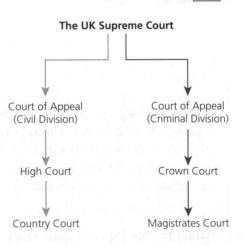

The UK Supreme Court

Court of Appeal (Civil Division) → High Court → Country Court

Court of Appeal (Criminal Division) → Crown Court → Magistrates Court

Judgements made in court can still be overruled by superior courts. Parliament can always change the law, and then the courts must follow that statute rather than the previous precedent.

Advantages of precedent	Disadvantages of precedent
Certainty: the rule that lower courts are bound by higher courts makes the law clear. **Practical rules:** precedent is based on real cases. **Evaluation of individual cases:** courts follow good precedent but try to avoid having to apply unfair or unworkable decisions.	**Complexity and volume:** the huge volume of cases going back over 400 years means it can be very difficult to find an appropriate precedent. **Out of touch:** there is always a danger that old cases are followed and not updated. **Conflicting precedents:** different decisions that have been made on the same topic can make judges' decisions unpredictable. **Chance:** judges develop the law via precedent, but cases are brought to court by chance, and therefore the speed at which development of the law occurs is also left to chance. **Social consequences:** judges have no way of researching the social consequences of the decisions they make; they can only make decisions based on the evidence presented.

Interpreting statutes

Parliament creates statutes but it is left to courts to interpret them. This can prove very difficult as when statutes are drafted it is impossible to think about every eventuality for which they will be used. Courts try to interpret statues very literally but as this is unlikely to produce the most appropriate results, courts usually use the purposive approach, i.e. they try to establish what purpose the statute intended to achieve.

The powers of the courts — Revised

The courts have extensive powers to make orders in civil cases.

Civil court orders	
Damages	Intended to compensate the claimant for the actions of the defendant. Usual remedy in cases of: ● **tort:** damages are intended to put the claimant in the same position as if the tort had not been committed ● contract cases: damages are intended to put the claimant in the same position, as far as money can, as if the contract had been performed by the defendant.
Specific performance	An order made by a court telling the defendant to perform the terms of a contract. It is discretionary which means the court is never bound to grant it; it is never granted where damages would be sufficient.
Injunction	A discretionary remedy which allows a court to make an order restraining the defendant from breaking a contract or continuing to act in a way that would constitute a tort (i.e. an injunction might freeze a defendant's assets to prevent them leaving the country to avoid paying damages to a claimant).
Rescission	A discretionary remedy that allows a court to order that a contract be set aside in order to restore parties to the position they were in before it was made.
Rectification	Also discretionary, it allows the court to amend a document to reflect what the parties had originally intended it to express. This remedy can be used when a written document does not express the true agreement of the parties.
Declaration	This is a remedy asked of the court by a claimant to clarify what the law is on a disputed point.

Tort – a civil wrong committed by an individual against another where the defendant owed a duty to the claimant, was in breach of that duty and consequently caused loss or damage.

Examiner tip

Ensure you are clear about the differences between the powers of the civil courts and the criminal courts as this is also useful when analysing the difference between criminal law and civil law.

N.B. Discretionary remedies are only used in limited circumstances where damages would not be an appropriate remedy.

In criminal cases, the purpose of the law is to punish those who have been convicted. The judges do this by giving out sentences.

Criminal court sentences	
Custodial sentences	Time spent in prison. The judge decides on the length of sentencing based on guidelines and short custodial sentences can be suspended for between six months and two years. The judge may not use his or her discretion when sentencing an offender for murder – a life sentence must be at least fifteen years in length.
Fines and fixed penalties	An order to pay money to the state – **this money does not go to the victim of the crime**. Fines are the most common sentence and Magistrates' Courts usually only fine up to £5000. Fixed penalties refers to set financial penalties like parking tickets or 'on the spot fines' and these can be applied without using the court system.
Community sentences	These sentences are intended to leave an offender in the community but restrict their freedoms. They might involve unpaid work, compulsory drug/alcohol rehabilitation, mental health treatment or a curfew.
Other miscellaneous sentences	These include: ● Mental health orders: detaining those with serious mental health disorders in a hospital for treatment. ● Binding over to be of good behaviour: money is put up as a bond of good behaviour. ● Conditional discharge: no action is taken unless offender commits another crime for no more than three years. ● Absolute discharge: no action is taken against the defendant because even though a crime has been committed it would be inappropriate to impose a punishment.

Now test yourself

Tested ☐

1 What is the 'purposive approach'?
2 Identify the powers that civil courts have.
3 Explain some of the issues that courts have when balancing conflicting rights.
4 Assess the advantages and disadvantages of precedent.

Answers on p.108

Examiner tip

Remember: the highest court in the UK is the Supreme Court (although on matters of EU law it is the European Court of Justice). Until 2009 it was the House of Lords but the **Constitutional Reform Act 2005** created the Supreme Court in an attempt to try to separate the judicial function (interpreting law) of the House of Lords with its legislative function (creating law).

8.2 The courts and the Human Rights Act

Civil actions to enforce human rights

Revised ☐

How did the Human Rights Act affect civil actions in the UK?

Although the UK had ratified the European Convention on Human Rights in 1951, it was not part of UK law which meant UK courts could not apply its terms. The HRA makes it possible to use any UK court to seek a remedy for a breach of rights by a public authority under the ECHR. It also means that British Courts can rule that an existing law is incompatible with the ECHR – meaning that Parliament will then have to change it.

Websites

UK Supreme Court website with details of current cases and decided cases: www.supremecourt.gov.uk

Case study 1 *Thompson and Venables v News Group Newspapers Ltd (2001)*

In 1993, two ten-year-old boys, Jon Venables and Robert Thompson, abducted, tortured and murdered a two-year-old, James Bulger. They were convicted of his murder and served eight years in young offender units. The trial judge ordered injunctions to prevent details about their life and identities being published, as this may have jeopardised their safety. Several newspapers sought to lift the injunction citing a breach of Article 10 of the European Convention on Human Rights (right to freedom of expression) including the News Group named above. The court believed there was evidence that if the injunction were lifted the lives of Venables and Thompson would be at risk and the injunctions remained under Article 2 (right to life).

Case study 2 · *Douglas v Hello! Ltd (2001)*

In 2000, Catherine Zeta-Jones and Michael Douglas, both famous Hollywood actors, married in a hotel in New York. They agreed a £1 million deal with *OK!* magazine to publish exclusive pictures of their wedding. They put security in place and took any photographic equipment from guests to ensure that no other photographers obtained access to their wedding or reception. However, *Hello!* magazine managed to acquire photographs and published

them. Zeta-Jones and Douglas argued that their right to privacy under the Human Rights Act had been breached. It was argued that the Human Rights Act did not apply to the case because *Hello!* magazine was not a public authority but the Court held that as the Court itself was a form of public authority it was therefore unable to ignore the provisions of the HRA. The case was therefore able to succeed.

Case study 3 · *Othman v UK*

Abu Qatada (also known as Omar Mahmoud Othman) is a Jordanian citizen, granted asylum in the UK in 1994 on grounds of religious persecution. He is an Islamic militant and believed by several governments to be involved in terrorism. In 2002, he was imprisoned in the UK for suspected terrorist activity. The British Government then attempted to

deport him to Jordan to face charges; however, Abu Qatada claims he will not receive a fair trial in Jordan and may face torture. After a lengthy legal battle the European Court of Human Rights ruled that it would be a breach of Article 6 (right to fair trial). Abu Qatada was therefore allowed to remain in the UK and released under strict bail conditions in February 2012.

Remedies for breach of rights protected by the ECHR

`Revised`

It is important to note that if a breach of an individual's rights is also a crime (e.g. assault) then criminal proceedings can be brought against the perpetrator of the crime either by the state or by the individual as a private prosecution. However, under private prosecution there is no guarantee that an individual will be awarded any financial benefit from fines imposed as these will go to the state.

> **Habeas corpus** Latin term meaning 'let us have the body'. A person who has been detained has the right to question the legality of their detention. Applicants for Habeas corpus take priority over all other business in court.

Remedy	Details
European Court of Human Rights	Although the Human Rights Act allows an individual to seek remedy for violations of rights under the European Convention on Human Rights via any British court, it is important to appreciate that if they exhaust the appeal system in the UK (by appealing all the way up to the Supreme Court), or the Supreme Court has set a precedent it is unlikely to overturn, they can still take their case to the European Court of Human Rights in Strasbourg. After a judgement of the European Court of Human Rights, a case can also then be referred to the Grand Chamber for reconsideration.
Ombudsman	The ombudsman can investigate any breach of an individual's rights that falls within their remit, including rights under the ECHR.
Judicial review	The process by which an individual can ask a court to decide if a public body has acted lawfully or not. It is an important way of enforcing rights when a public authority has acted outside of the powers it has been given.
Habeas corpus	This is exercised by the Divisional Court of the Queen's Bench of the High Court. It can be used by suspects being held by the police during investigation and those placed in custody pending trial.
Self-defence	In theory, every citizen has the right to use reasonable force to protect themselves from any unlawful interference by another (criminal or civil). It can be very difficult in reality to employ this remedy as the judgement as to whether force is reasonable rather than excessive can be difficult to prove. Use of excessive force may actually result in a conviction for a citizen seeking to protect themselves.

The Role of the UK Supreme Court and the European Court of Human Rights

- The Supreme Court was created in 2009. It removed the role of the House of Lords as the highest court in the land and therefore allowed the judiciary to be more separate from Parliament (legislature).

- It better ensures the right to a fair trial if the judiciary can remain more separate from the legislature. For example, the Supreme Court might be ruling on a piece of legislature that its members had a role in creating.

- The Supreme Court must give effect to the rights contained in the European Convention on Human Rights.

- It must take account of any decision made by the European Court of Human Rights and should not dilute any ruling unless they have very good reason.

- Any citizen that feels that their rights under the convention have been breached by a UK court, or the Supreme Court itself, can take a case against the UK to the European Court of Human Rights.

Websites

The European Court of Human Rights website which contains information on judgements:
www.echr.coe.int

Now test yourself

 Tested

1 Briefly explain two case studies concerning civil actions to enforce human rights.
2 Outline the remedies available to an individual for breach of rights protected by the ECHR.
3 How did the Human Rights Act change existing routes of redress for breaches of human rights?
4 Assess the advantages of the Supreme Court.

Answers on p.108

Typical mistake

Students sometimes misunderstand what constitutes a public body in the context of the Human Rights Act protecting citizens against breaches of their human rights by public bodies. A public body is widely defined but includes central and local government, the police, the NHS and the courts.

8.3 Judicial review

The purpose and extent of judicial review

What is judicial review?

Judicial review refers to the power that the High Court has to review the exercise of public power on behalf of a citizen. This means that the Court is able to decide whether an action of a public body is lawful or not. This allows a person who has been adversely affected by a decision of a public body to ask the Court to review the decision. Its purpose is to ensure that the rights of citizens are protected against the powers exercised by the state (via public bodies).

Who can apply for judicial review?

- When making an application for judicial review, the applicant must have a sufficient interest in the matter and must therefore have a close connection to the subject. This is to prevent vexatious litigants (those who want to bring actions to harass public bodies or waste time). Some pressure groups and interest groups are considered to have such an interest even though they are not personally involved.

- The Attorney General (chief law officer of the government) is presumed always to have an interest and can allow any action to go ahead under his or her name.

- Decisions made by the Parliamentary Commissioner for Standards are exempt from judicial review as they are part of the proceedings of parliament, which is not subject to review by the courts.

- Rights protected by private law (arising from a contract or tort) cannot be the subject of judicial review – a remedy for a breach of rights under private law would have to be sought via civil courts.

Judicial review and natural justice

Revised

When a citizen uses judicial review to ask a court to decide if an action of a public body was lawful or not, they can only do so under the following situations:

Substantive *ultra vires*	A public body makes a decision that it does not have the power to make.
Procedural *ultra vires*	A public body does not use the correct procedure for making a decision or shows bias or unfairness in making a decision.
Unreasonableness	A public body makes a decision that is unreasonable. In assessing unreasonableness the Court must consider the 'Wednesbury Principles' based on a previous case involving a Corporation of that name. These principles assert that examples of unreasonableness include: - the public authority has taken into account matters that were irrelevant - the public authority has made the decision for an improper purpose - the public authority must exercise discretion when making rules rather than creating wide-ranging rules to apply to all cases.
Natural justice	A public body makes a decision that is in breach of natural justice. **Natural justice** dictates that the powers and duties of public authorities are exercised following the rules of 'fair play'. When deciding if a public body making the decision was biased, a court should: - identify all circumstances that had an effect on the suggestion that the decision was biased, and - determine whether or not those circumstances would lead a fair-minded and informed observer to conclude there was a real possibility that the body was biased.

ultra vires – Latin term that literally means 'beyond the powers'.

Natural justice – concept held within the legal systems of all democratic countries that certain principles are fundamental to any decision-making process. The two main rules are:

- no one should be a judge in their own case (decisions should be made without bias)
- both sides have a right to be heard.

Remedies available through judicial review

Remedy	Details
Damages, injunction and declaration	As in a civil action: Damages – the payment of compensation. Injunction – an order preventing the defendant from some act. Declaration – a statement of the law and rights and responsibilities of the parties.
The following are only available in judicial review proceedings and are discretionary:	
Quashing Order	Quashes the decision of a public body that has been called into question by judicial review.
Mandatory Order	An order to an inferior court or public body telling it to do something.
Prohibiting Order	This order prevents a tribunal or a public authority from doing something that could be subject to a quashing order, for example it could be used to prevent a tribunal from starting proceedings that are outside of its jurisdiction.

Criticisms of the judicial review process

Criticisms	Details
'Wednesbury Principles' are too strict	The test for unreasonableness used as a result of the Wednesbury case is too restrictive. The European Court of Human Rights has been critical in the past of this test for unreasonableness.
It may be difficult to establish the extent of a public body's power	Public bodies are often given the choice about whether or not to use the power it has been given, and they are also often wide ranging. Trying to ascertain what is and is not within the powers of a public body may be very difficult.
Decisions made by judicial review are often of a political nature	Many judicial reviews concern the questioning of a minister's decision as head of a government department (public body). Those decisions can often be politically motivated as ministers usually belong to political parties with very clear agendas. Some commentators believe that the courts are more likely to agree with the decisions made by the ministers of Conservative governments.
Decisions relating to national security	Some critics argue that when a judicial review concerns a matter of national security, courts are reluctant to assess the strength of evidence provided by the state or even consider whether decisions made were rational. This could possibly be due to fears that scrutiny of the state's actions in such matters might risk national security.

Now test yourself

1 What is the purpose of judicial review?
2 In which situations can judicial review occur?
3 Outline the remedies available through judicial review.
4 Assess the effectiveness of judicial review.

Answers on pp.108–109

Exam practice

Assess the advantages **and** disadvantages of the new UK Supreme Court. **(15 marks)**

Answers and quick quiz online

Chapter 9 Who holds power in the UK?

9.1 The concept and nature of power

Power, authority, influence, democracy and mandate

Term	Description	Examples
Power	The ability to control or influence people.	Economic power of a major multinational company. The power of a trade union. The power of the media. Power resides in these bodies, organisations and people due to their position within a society.
Authority	The ability to exercise power legitimately, i.e. with legal entitlement. The citizen recognises and accepts that the person or institution has legitimate authority over them. The term 'authority' is often interchanged with 'power'. For example, 'political power' is used to mean that a person/party has the political authority to do something. The term 'authority' can also be used in the context of moral authority, where the status of an individual/ group implies to others that they have the position or understanding of an issue to speak out on a matter.	A police constable has the authority to arrest you. Parliament has authority and legitimacy through being elected to pass laws in regard to you.
Influence	In the context of citizenship this relates to the belief that an individual/group is able to ensure that those in power take account of their views, due to their own position or power. It is perceived by others that these views are acted on. This term is often used and interchanged with power.	Politicians are influenced in their views by the way in which the media respond to their proposals.
Democracy	A political system where ultimate power resides with the people/electorate to determine the way they are governed.	A democratic system allows its citizens to be able to: ● elect candidates at elections ● vote freely for the person of their choice ● vote in secret. ● It has regular free and open elections. A democratic system is where government is accountable to the people at all levels.
Mandate	This is a term that often gets confused with 'manifesto'. A mandate is an endorsement by those who are consulted or vote upon an issue. The term is generally used in relation to the election of a government.	If a party has a majority of the seats in the UK Parliament after an election, they claim to have a mandate from the people to carry out their manifesto. If a group of protesters held a meeting and had a vote and decided to take a form of action their leaders would claim to have a mandate for that action (approval by the body they represent).

Power and the state

- In a democracy, when a government is formed after a general election, that government has a mandate to introduce its policies, providing it can achieve a majority in parliament to pass the necessary legislation.

- In the UK, the power of the state is theoretically absolute. It can pass laws in regards to any aspect of life, e.g. close down local government, nationalise banks, remove the judicial system, abolish the monarchy.

- There are checks and balances on the power of a government. The UK Supreme Court powers include the right to determine whether laws conflict with the Human Rights Act 1998.

- As a member of the EU, many laws in the UK result from EU decisions and regulations.

- In the UK system of government, the House of Lords may seek to amend or delay legislation. However, ultimately the government can use the Parliament Act to force through any legislation opposed by the House of Lords.

- Once legislation gains the Royal Assent, i.e. the Queen's approval, it becomes law. In theory the monarch can refuse to agree to a new law, but no monarch has done so for hundreds of years.

The nature of political power within the UK

The government of the UK operates at several levels. These levels of government are often referred to as Tiers.

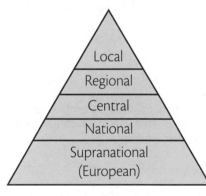

Local
Regional
Central
National
Supranational
(European)

> **Examiner tip**
>
> To help you remember the different tiers of UK government, think of the analogy of the tiers of a wedding cake: local, regional, central, national, supranational (European).

European Union: As a member, some political powers have been transferred to the EU. This is called 'shared sovereignty'. This transfer of power to the EU has become a major political issue for many politicians.

UK central government: Sovereignty within the UK system of government resides with the UK Parliament in London. All other tiers of government only exist as determined by the UK Parliament.

Devolved government: The term is used to describe **devolution**; the transfer of power from one body to another. In the case of the UK, this is the transfer of powers to Scotland, Wales and Northern Ireland.

> **Devolution** – the transfer of powers from one body to another.

Scotland: In Scotland there had not been a parliament since the Act of Union in 1707. In 1998 a referendum was held and Scotland voted for a Scottish parliament with the authority to have tax-varying powers and law-making powers.

Wales: In a 1997 referendum the people of Wales voted in favour of devolution. The Welsh were given an assembly with limited powers. Since then, further powers have been granted to the Welsh Assembly.

Northern Ireland: From 1921 until 1972 the people of Northern Ireland were largely governed by MPs elected to the Northern Ireland Parliament known as Stormont (after the building in which the parliament met). In 1972 the UK government disbanded the Northern Ireland Parliament and introduced direct UK rule as a result of civil unrest. As a result of the peace process and the Good Friday Agreement of 1998, devolved power was restored to Northern Ireland and an assembly has been established with law-making powers.

Local government: Also referred to as local council or local authority, this is the lowest level of government in the UK. It is responsible for the delivery of local community services. Central government determines the different types of local councils that exist, and determines their finances through central government grants. Local government also get income from council tax, a tax on people/property. Local government councils are made up of locally elected councillors who are paid an allowance.

As London is the capital city of the UK, it has always had a slightly different system of local government. Power is divided between the local areas (boroughs) and a central authority. From the mid 1980s until 1997, when Labour returned to government, there was no central London government body. Now there is the Greater London Authority (GLA) and the post of a directly elected mayor who is responsible for running local government services in London. Directly elected mayors are a recent innovation in local government in the UK. The majority of councils retain a ceremonial mayor/chairman, and appoint a leader of the council.

> **Websites**
>
> Parliament and government:
> www.parliament.uk/about/how/role/parliament-government
> Local Government website:
> www.localgov.co.uk/index.cfm
> Northern Ireland Assembly:
> www.niassembly.gov.uk
> The Scottish Parliament:
> www.scottish.parliament.uk
> The London Assembly:
> www.london.gov.uk
> Welsh Government: www.wales.gov.uk

Who holds political power in the UK?

Revised

The political system in the UK consists of competing political parties with differing ideologies (political ideas). These parties contest elections at every level of government in the UK. The UK also has a number of nationally based parties that only contest elections in their own countries, i.e. the Scottish Nationalist Party (SNP).

Political parties are made up of individual citizens who pay a subscription and join. Some of these citizens go on to become candidates for their party at local or parliamentary elections. Others hold office within the party and/or contribute to the development of party policy. Others campaign for the party in their local communities. The overall membership of political parties in the UK in recent years has been in decline.

Each of the major UK political parties is run in different ways:

The **Conservative Party** gives a lot of power and authority to its elected leader. Leaders are elected by the membership after Members of Parliament (MPs) ballot to produce two names to go forward. The leader gives political direction to the party and is responsible for policy formation. He/she decides whom they want in the shadow cabinet and who will hold office when they are in government.	The **Labour Party**, which was founded by the trade unions, has an Electoral College system in regard to electing its leader. Each section has a percentage of the vote and these votes are then aggregated to decide the winner. The three sections are: the MPs, the local party membership and the trade unions. In 2011 it was decided that the leader could decide the membership of the Labour shadow cabinet.	The **Liberal Democrats** members decide their leader in a secret ballot. Policy is decided at their annual conference on a basis of one person, one vote. The leader determines the membership of the Liberal Democrat shadow cabinet.

Case studies of the impact of the use of power on others

Revised

Recent cases that explain the use of political power:

- In the 2008 banking crisis, the government was forced to use its power to stabilise the banking system. It saved Northern Rock and took large shareholdings in Lloyds/TSB and Royal Bank of Scotland (RBS). Unless the government acted it was likely that the banking system would have collapsed.

- In 2010 the new coalition government decided that tuition fees for university students would rise. This led to massive demonstrations about the decision but even the protesters did not challenge the right of parliament to make the decision.

- In 2010 the United Nations agreed that military power could be used to defend the citizens of Libya from attack by their own government forces. The UK, France and others deployed through NATO aircraft and ships to protect civilians by bombing.

Websites

The Labour Party: www.labour.org.uk
The Conservative Party: www.conservativeparty.org.uk
The Liberal Democrats: www.libdems.org.uk
The Scottish Nationalist Party: www.snp.org.uk
Plaid Cymru: www.plaidcymru.org
Democratic Unionist Party: www.mydup.com
Sinn Féin: www.sinnfein.ie

Now test yourself

Tested

1 What is the difference between power and authority?
2 Which body holds ultimate power in the UK?
3 What is meant by the term 'devolution'?
4 Why is it claimed that the leader of the Conservative Party has more power than other party leaders?
5 What is a mandate?

Answers on p.109

Examiner tip

It is important that you can anchor your understanding of these concepts and ideas through the use of case studies. Try to ensure that any case studies you refer to when answering a question are reasonably current.

9.2 Who has economic power in the UK?

The concepts of economic power and control

Revised

In the context of citizenship, the term 'economic power' relates to organisations and corporate bodies that have an impact on the UK economy.

'Economic control' relates to the ways in which the state and any other bodies seek to control those who have economic power.

Examiner tip

It is important to remember the ways in which the UK economy is interrelated with the EU and the wider world economy.

 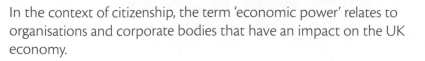 Exam practice answers and quick quizzes at **www.therevisionbutton.co.uk/myrevisionnotes**

Some examples of economic control are where government has:

- passed legislation to regulate the powers of trade unions
- established bodies like the Competition Commission to regulate company takeovers
- passed legislation in regard to a national minimum wage.

Websites

The Competition Commission:
www.competition-commission.org.uk/

Trades Union Congress:
www.tuc.org.uk

Economic power of the state   Revised

Countries organise and control their economies in differing ways.

Three broad classifications are:

- A **planned economy** is where the state controls the output of the economy and usually exercises state ownership over the means of production. This style of management was associated with the former communist countries.
- A **mixed economy** is where there is both an element of the economy owned and controlled by the state and an element in private ownership.
- A **free market economy** is where limited services are provided by the state, provision is left to private companies and there is limited state regulation.

The UK economy has been traditionally labeled as a mixed economy, which means neither the government nor businesses control all the economic activities of the country – both sectors play an important role in economic decision-making. Some elements of the economy are in public ownership and some are in private ownership. However, during the Second World War, the UK government exercised almost total control over all aspects of the economy.

Since 1979, the UK has moved towards a 'free market' economy, where the government moves away from direct ownership to establishing a regulatory role. The USA has been traditionally labeled a 'free market' economy.

The UK government, like others, is constrained in the extent to which they can intervene in economic issues because of its membership of international bodies such as the EU and the World Trade Organisation.

Here are some examples of actions that a government could take in regards to the economy. All of these actions have been taken by UK governments since 1945:

- nationalisation – the state taking over the ownership of a company from a private owner
- de-nationalisation – selling government-owned assets to the private sector, also known as 'privatisation'
- raising and lowering levels of personal income tax
- introducing new taxes
- price controls over ranges of products
- ordering pay freezes
- attempting to fix the value of the pound
- raising and lowering the bank rate (interest rates)
- legislating about trade union activity
- establishing regulators to determine price levels in certain industries.

The concept of economic power at a local, regional, national, European and global level

Revised

Locally, the economy may be:

- dominated by a sole employer
- heavily reliant on public sector employment
- reliant on one sector of the economy, e.g. agriculture, mining or fishing.

Regionally, the economy may be reliant on one sector of the economy, for example the Midlands is associated with industrial production, and the City of London is associated with financial services.

Nationally, the UK is currently attempting to restructure its economy from an over reliance upon the service sector, especially financial services, to manufacturing.

At an EU level many decisions are made which impact on the economies of member states. The EU is working towards a single market where the movement of goods and services is not hindered by individual national government regulation. Already EU citizens can live and work in other member countries and have their qualifications recognised.

At a global level, bodies such as the World Trade Organisation (WTO) and the International Monetary Fund (IMF) can impact upon the economy of individual countries and ensure that certain actions are taken.

> **Examiner tip**
>
> Remember that beyond the national level, governments choose to join international bodies and by their membership agree to be a part of their decision-making processes by that action, they agree to pool or share elements of their economic or political sovereignty.

> **Typical mistake**
>
> Make sure you are aware of the scope of the powers of the EU. Many students write as if the EU impacts on every aspect of life in the UK. They also particularly confuse Human Rights legislation, which derives from the Council of Europe and the European Court of Human Right in Strasbourg; with the EU and its Court of Justice which is based in Luxembourg.

Trading, fiscal and monetary responsibilities

Revised

Trading responsibilities

The UK government ensures that the voice of the UK is heard and its interests are protected when it is involved in international discussions regarding trade issues. As a member of the EU, the UK was very keen that the Doha round of talks regarding international free trade was successful, but other countries felt their economies would suffer so therefore no agreement was signed.

Monetary responsibilities

In 1997, the UK government decided that the power that the Chancellor of the Exchequer had to set the Bank of England interest rates should be handed over to an independent group called the Monetary Policy Committee (MPC) of the Bank of England. The MPC has a mandate to set UK interest rates in order to deliver a set level of **inflation**.

> **Inflation** – a general, continuous rise in prices and/or wages.

Fiscal responsibilities

Fiscal policy is about the ways in which the government raises and spends its income to support the economy.

- If government income is in excess of its spending, the government is said to be operating surplus.
- If government spending is in excess of its income, it is said to be running a deficit.

The deficit that a government has is met by borrowing from financial markets. Following the financial crisis of 2008/9, the UK deficit increased dramatically, as did the deficit of many other countries. Subsequently, some countries have now found it difficult to borrow money at a reasonable cost.

> **Websites**
>
> The UK Treasury indicating the current pattern of UK government spending and its sources of income:
> www.hm-treasury.gov.uk/budget.htm

The role of the financial sector including banks and banking

Revised

- The UK banking sector is the third largest in the world after the USA and Japan.
- 95 per cent of the UK population use banking services.
- The banking sector currently employs 3.5 per cent of the UK's workforce.
- Banks contribute nearly 7 per cent to the total UK Gross Domestic Product (GDP).
- The UK financial sector is a major international player and accounts for 20 per cent of all global lending with UK banks dealing with a third of all global foreign exchange business.

> **Examiner tip**
>
> The financial sector also includes insurance companies and pension funds, both of which are major investors in the UK economy and sources of government borrowing.

The role of government and the Bank of England

Revised

- The Bank of England has been the government's banker since 1694 and was the body that oversaw government borrowing requirements.
- In current terminology, the Bank of England is the UK's central bank in the same way as the Federal Reserve Bank is in America, and the Bundesbank is in Germany.
- The Governor of the Bank of England is appointed by the government, although the post is not seen as a party political appointment.
- With the establishment of the MPC (see page 64), the monthly decision regarding the bank rate level is eagerly monitored and the minutes of the meeting, published ten days later, are closely followed.
- Following the banking crisis, the Bank of England has been given increased regulatory powers regarding the banking sector. These new powers have come about by changes to the role of the Financial Services Authority (FSA).
- The Bank of England publishes regular reports on the state of the UK economy and has regional offices throughout the UK.

The economic power of companies: local, national and multinational

Revised

Within a market economy, the role of the private sector is very important with regards to employment creation and investment. In a local area or region, the actions of an individual company can have a dramatic impact on the local economy, for example the recent resurgence of the UK motor industry while in foreign ownership has seen job creation in the Sunderland area and the West Midlands and Oxford. This is due to expansion plans by Nissan, Land Rover/Jaguar and Mini whose parent companies are Japanese, Indian and German.

> **Examiner tip**
>
> Look at case studies of the impact on local communities in the 1980s and 1990s of coal mine and steel work closures and the decline in motorcar production to help you understand the impact of decline on a local economy.

Multinational companies

- Many UK companies are also worldwide brands, for example Tesco, which controls 30 per cent of the UK retail food market and is important in many overseas countries.
- Major UK companies can also have an impact on their own supply chain, often attempting to raise quality and decrease costs to consumers.
- The UK government is proposing legislation to protect agricultural producers to ensure they receive fair prices and contracts for their goods.

- Every high street in the UK and abroad seems to contain similar shop signs and sell similar products. This is seen by many as a negative impact of globalisation, as these businesses often have a negative impact on local producers.
- Some internationally global companies are welcomed by governments, for example global companies have set up car manufacturing factories in the UK, such as Nissan which runs one of the most successful car plants in the world in Sunderland, and Honda which has major plants in Swindon.
- Often governments have to compete with each other to attract overseas investment. Within the EU, any package offered to an investor must be approved by the EU to ensure that there is a level playing field between member states.

Economic power and the citizen as employer, employee and customer

Revised

A citizen takes on a number of roles within the economy, and in each role they have economic power:

Role within economy	Economic power
Consumer of goods and services	The purchase or lack of purchase of goods can lead to economic growth or decline.
	Actions can impact upon individual companies, for example consumer **boycotts** can lead to companies failing.
	During the financial crisis, customers queuing to take their money out of Northern Rock quickly led to the demise of the bank.
Employer/ Employee	The citizen undertakes certain responsibilities towards the state and contributes through taxation.

When citizens work together they can often have an impact on the economy. Public sector strikes by unions can lead to schools and other public sector offices being closed.

> **Boycotts** – refusal to deal with a particular organisation, commonly by refusing to buy products or use services.

Case studies about the impact of the use of economic power

Revised

An example of the impact of an individual citizen on economic power is the impact of the campaign led by Rebecca Hosking regarding the use of plastic bags in shops. Initially she convinced traders in her local town of Modbury, Devon to use non-plastic bags. Through the internet, the campaign became worldwide. Politicians noticed the campaign, as did major retailers, and now the public are aware of the issues of plastic bag pollution.

> **Websites**
>
> How Green Are You: Information about the plastic bag campaign: www.channel4.com/lifestyle/green/green-people/hosking.html

Now test yourself

Tested

1 What is the difference between a mixed economy and free market economy?
2 Identify three ways a government can intervene in their economy.
3 What is the difference between monetary policy and fiscal policy?
4 Why are financial services important to the UK economy?
5 What is the MPC?

Answers on p.109

9.3 What is the influence of the media and how is its power controlled?

What are the media (broadcasting, newspapers and other media)?

Media, or mass media, relates to a range of differing forms of presenting information, news and opinion to a large number of people at the same time.

Over time, the nature of mass media has changed, and it is still evolving. Traditionally the term only related to newspapers and magazines. The advent of radio and television broadened the definition. Today phrases like 'traditional media', 'e-media' or 'new media' are used. E-media relates to web-based formats. The term 'social media' has recently come into use to describe how individual citizens can generate news, opinion and set the agenda.

> **Media** – this term now encompasses formats like e-media and social media as well as traditional formats like the press and broadcasting.

> **Websites**
>
> The most popular newspapers in the UK: www.mediauk.com/article/32696/the-most-popular-newspapers-in-the-uk

How public opinion is created

The traditional media used to be perceived as having the ability to set the public agenda on a range of issues. They provided the public with the evidence on which they could arrive at an opinion through investigative journalism, placement of the story and continuing interest in the event. Being in private ownership, newspapers have been able to pursue some stories that suit their own agenda.

However, with the development of new media formats, setting the agenda for public opinion now has much wider ownership. Events during the 'Arab Spring' only came to light because of the power of 'citizen journalists' who used the latest internet technology and social networking sites to tell their story to a worldwide audience. Also, the increase in viewers having access to satellite television, or freeview, ensures that there are now more sources of television news than previously.

The government requires that public broadcasters on radio and television have to be politically neutral, that they should have high reporting standards and can be held to account.

> **Examiner tip**
>
> When answering questions about the media ensure that you mention a range of differing formats of both traditional and e-media.

Media ownership and control

There have been major debates in the UK about the concentration of media ownership, originally regarding mainly newspapers, but today regarding cross-media ownership involving several different platforms.

Any media takeovers are subject to government supervision and EU regulations to ensure that no single company has a dominant position within any market. This can be seen in the case of the News International bid to take over the part of BSkyB that it did not own. This was approved by the EU, but News International later withdrew their bid.

> **Typical mistake**
>
> When answering questions about media, some students make mistakes which normally revolve around misreading questions and either writing about one format of media only or writing generically about the media without using examples. If the term 'media' is used in the question, ensure you write about a range of formats.

Globalisation of the media

Revised

Globalisation of the media relates to the ownership of traditional media sources across several countries. Increasingly, companies like News International are part of major international corporations. Programmes made by the company, or sports events that have been purchased by them, can be used across a variety of platforms to generate income. The vast amount of money that is paid to the Premier League for televising their matches is repaid by viewers and advertisers across the world. The interest from Asia in UK football has resulted in the sale of team-endorsed items and interest from Asian citizens in purchasing clubs.

The globalisation of the media in a 24-hour news agenda ensures that anything happening anywhere can be made known to millions within minutes. In the last few years, the growth in social media has allowed citizens to present stories, which can then be followed up by the traditional media. In 2012, a young pupil at primary school in Scotland established a blog to comment on the state of her school dinners. Within a few days the site became 'viral' (vast amount of interest shown) and over 1,000,000 people had visited the site.

> **Globalisation** – the term used to describe the process by which countries are becoming more interdependent and interconnected – specifically via communication links and trade. It is also used to describe how some companies are becoming global brands, i.e Coca-Cola and McDonald's.

Government and the media

Revised

The relationship of the government and politicians to newspapers formed part of the public inquiry led by Lord Leveson in 2011–12. The government has a duty to protect the public interest and has a direct interest in public service broadcasting (BBC). Through legislation it can have an impact upon the ownership and control of other media formats.

Increasingly the debate revolves around the relationship between politicians and the media. These are the issues that the Leveson Inquiry has investigated. Politicians wish the media to present their news story whether in opposition or government in order to help establish a public profile and to set the news agenda. Equally elements of the media, especially newspapers, often have an agenda or political viewpoint they wish to put forward. The issue is whether that relationship has been too close and how, if required, it should be regulated.

> **Websites**
>
> The government has a ministry entitled the Department of Media and Culture, which oversees the work of the media. For details of its work visit its website: www.culture.gov.uk/media/index.aspx

> **Examiner tip**
>
> For detailed evidence about this relationship look at samples of evidence on the Leveson Inquiry website: www.levesoninquiry.org.uk

Regulation of the media

Revised

We all benefit from the concept of 'freedom of press' and it is one that is held to be very important. However, it is important that the press is responsible so that individuals and groups can challenge anything that is reported in the media.

> **Websites**
>
> Information about self-regulation of the press: www.politics.co.uk/reference/self-regulation-of-the-press
> Ofcom: www.ofcom.org.uk/
> Information about Article 19, media regulation in the UK: www.article19.org/data/files/pdfs/publications/uk-media-regulation.pdf
> Press Complaints Commission: www.pcc.org.uk
> Copy of Royal Charter for the continuance of the BBC: www.bbc.co.uk/bbctrust/assets/files/pdf/about/how_we_govern/charter.pdf
> Advertising Standards Agency: www.asa.org.uk

The Press Complaints Commission (PCC)	The PCC currently regulates the press. This is a voluntary industry-based body, so, for example, the Express group of newspapers does not belong to the PCC. It has established a code of conduct and can investigate complaints from individuals and recommend forms of redress. However, its powers are not mandatory.
Ofcom	Ofcom is a government-established regulator for the communications industry. It ensures the public are protected against harmful and offensive material. It also has a legal supervisory role in regard to regulation. The former Independent Broadcasting Authority, which regulated the independent terrestrial channels, has now been absorbed into Ofcom.
The BBC Charter	The BBC is governed by a charter which is subject to parliamentary approval. It established the licence fee arrangements and the range of services the BBC can provide. The charter was last reviewed in 2006. The BBC has its own complaints website: www.bbc.co.uk/complaints.
Advertising Standards Authority (ASA)	The ASA is independent of both the government and the advertising industry but is recognised by the government, the courts and other regulators such as Ofcom as the body to deal with complaints about advertising.

Political 'spin'

Revised ☐

Political spin is the ability of a politician or their spokesperson to introduce a story to the news media and then attempt to put their own interpretation on that story, seeking to convince reporters or a live audience of that interpretation.

The issue of political spin was the centre of a major public debate regarding the publication of a government information document in the lead up to the Iraq War in 2003. The media portrayed the views that were put forward by the government in the document as the 'dodgy dossier'.

> **Examiner tip**
>
> Answers relating to this area should not rely heavily upon reference to the ASA as this deals only with the content of advertisements.

The influence of the media on political attitudes of citizens

Revised ☐

The media can appear to influence the political attitudes of citizens due to the nature of having large audiences and the ability to feature and repeat news and stories. The press in particular have led many successful campaigns that had led to change, for example the *Sunday Times* and the cases of Thalidomide in 1979. Today we have a range of media formats, so the ability of traditional media to establish an 'agenda' has decreased.

During the 2010 General Election newspapers in the UK declared for the following political parties:

Newspaper	Political party
The *Sun*	Conservatives
The *Daily Mirror*	Liberal Democrats
The *Daily Mail*	Conservatives
The *Daily Telegraph*	Conservatives
The *Times*	Conservatives
The *Guardian*	Liberal Democrats

The *Sun*, after several general elections, has claimed that it made the difference on behalf of the winning party. From 1979 until 1992 it supported the Conservative Party and from 1997 until 2010 supported the Labour Party. In 2010 it supported the Conservative Party. There is a question over whether the *Sun*'s support gave power to the party that they supported, or whether they endorsed what was likely to happen anyway and followed public opinion.

A very large section of the UK press is hostile to both the EU and the Euro and gives prominence to stories that support this hostile viewpoint. When polled about political issues that are important, respondents place the EU very low down on their list of priorities.

Websites

The Daily Mail and the murder of Stephen Lawrence: www.dailymail.co.uk/news/article-2080159/Stephen-Lawrence-case-How-killers-finally-brought-justice.html

From the European Commission: 'British think EU press reporting is too negative': http://ec.europa.eu/unitedkingdom/press/press_releases/2009/pr0998_en.htm

Now test yourself

Tested

1 Identify with examples three different types of media format.
2 Why is media ownership an issue?
3 Identify one media-led campaign in recent years that brought about change.
4 What does 'agenda setting' mean?
5 What is political 'spin'?

Answers on pp.109–110

Exam practice

Power in the UK is ultimately held by the electorate.
Discuss. **(15 marks)**

Answers and quick quiz online

Online

Examiner tip

A 15 mark question requires a short essay-style response. You need to ask yourself what are the key elements of the question. In this case the question is about the concept of power and its link to an electorate. In the UK there are regular parliamentary and other elections. The outcome of these elections determines who is in power, so the argument then can be made that power resides with the people (the electorate). Responses which gain higher marks may say that differing electoral systems produce different results and that the elector can only exercise power where they live and vote not nationally and many seats are safe for one party or another. In general elections it is not unknown for the party with most votes not to win the largest number of seats.

Chapter 10 The citizen and political power in the United Kingdom

10.1 The nature of government and its impact on the lives of citizens

The role of government and the different levels of government in the UK

Revised

The role of government

In its broadest sense, the role of government is to work within the constitution of the state:

- to provide for the security and defence of the nation
- to provide protection for its citizens
- to provide a legal, economic and social framework for the development of society
- to provide resolutions to issues as they emerge.

This role is also closely linked to the concept of sovereignty, whereby a nation state has control over its own affairs. Increasingly, states share or pool sovereignty to achieve policy objectives, e.g. the UK belongs to the EU, NATO and the UN, all of which can involve pooling or sharing sovereignty.

A narrower definition of government relates to the role of specific governments to be able to carry out the policies they have put forward in their election manifesto.

The functions of governments have greatly increased since 1900. Governments have become involved in providing welfare services, a social security system, education provision, increased local government services and health services.

The different levels of government

Central government in the UK involves the monarchy, Parliament and the judiciary. Parliament comprises both the House of Commons and the House of Lords. The government is formed after a General Election from Members of Parliament. It can be helpful to view the structure of government in the UK like an inverted pyramid:

Websites

Parliament and government: www.parliament.uk/about/how/role/parliament-government

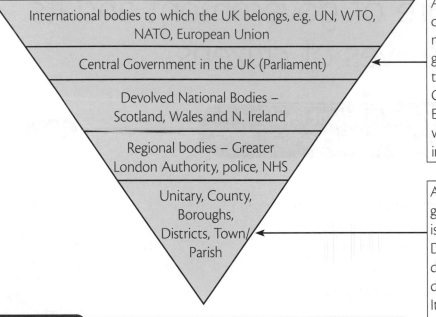

International bodies to which the UK belongs, e.g. UN, WTO, NATO, European Union

Central Government in the UK (Parliament)

Devolved National Bodies – Scotland, Wales and N. Ireland

Regional bodies – Greater London Authority, police, NHS

Unitary, County, Boroughs, Districts, Town/ Parish

All the levels of government above central government are optional and membership was a decision made by government. In 1973, the UK decided to join the then European Economic Community (EEC) now known as the EU. The government could decide to withdraw from the EU or any other international body to which we belong.

All the levels below central government only exist because it is the will of central government. Different levels of government have different powers and these are determined by central government. It is not possible for every level of government to deliver every type of service. A parish council would not be able to organise and equip a local army, and central government does not wish to organise the collection of your rubbish bins, hence the different levels/tiers of government.

Examiner tip

You need to be aware of the broad concepts involved in the different levels of government, and you need to be able to explain each concept and relate the concept to an example.

How government and its actions impact on the lives of citizens

Government imposes both rights and responsibilities on citizens through its actions.

- From the moment you are born, the state determines whether or not you meet the criteria for being a citizen of the state. Your birth has to be legally registered.

- The state provides social and welfare provision for you prior to birth and until death via the National Health Service (NHS), social security system, the benefit system, the education system and holds a general duty of care in regard to your welfare.

- As a citizen you have a duty to respect the laws of the country, to pay taxes that are due and, if

selected, to take part in the judicial process as a juror.

- Through the imposition of laws, regulation and taxation policy, government can impact upon every aspect of your life. The government could impose compulsory military service for all, re-introduce capital punishment for a range of crimes, legalise drugs, ban certain newspapers or television channels, fix all wages or introduce high levels of taxation.

Through its democratic mandate, the government of the day in the UK has immense power to impact upon our daily lives, but within a democracy, citizens judge the actions a government takes at the next general election.

Case study of services provided by differing levels of government

Level of government	Example of provider	Outline of the service	Why at this level?
Central Government	UK Government	Defence	Other levels of government could not sustain the costs. The integrity of the state could be comprised if there were competing forces.
National/ Devolved	Scotland	Higher Education	As a part of the devolution settlement, higher education was made a responsibility of the Scottish Parliament. It is not suited to lower levels of government due to where universities might be based. One local council could have two universities within its borders and another could have none. This devolved power has led to differences between Scotland and England, e.g. funding students in Higher Education differently.
Regional	London	Public Transport	As a large metropolitan city, is it important that the transport infrastructure is co-ordinated and investment is planned across the entire network. This would be very difficult to achieve if transport was the responsibility of the London Boroughs.
Local	Unitary	Social Services	Unitary councils are councils that exercise all the powers of local government in a given area. In many parts of the country there is still a tiered system of District and County councils working side by side, each with different responsibilities. County councils provide help to numerous vulnerable people of all ages. District or parish councils wouldn't have the ability to raise the money required or offer the range of services required. Central government would not have sufficient knowledge to deal with local needs.
Local	Parish/Town	Allotments	Allotments are areas of public land given over to people who wish to garden. The costs involved are limited and decisions about meeting local needs are best met at a very local level.

Examiner tip

For this element of the course, it is a good idea to make your own chart like the one above to ensure you can remember named case studies for services provided by each different level of government.

Typical mistake

Too often, responses are generic where students write in an abstract way about government. Always ensure that you embed examples in your response. You should research the work of local councils in your area.

Now test yourself

1 What type of constitution exists in the UK?
2 Define the term 'sovereignty'.
3 Identify three ways in which the government has impacted upon your life to date.
4 Why is defence policy best determined at a national level?
5 Identify one responsibility of UK citizens.

Answers on p.110

10.2 Local democracy

The structure of government within the UK

In the UK, political power is held by central government. It determines the nature of political power that is devolved to other bodies within the UK, for example assemblies or local authorities. These other bodies cannot act beyond the powers they have been granted by central government. Central government also maintains control in regard to local council spending as the bulk of local authority income comes from central government grants.

This section looks at the nature, role and responsibilities exercised by central and local government, and additionally the position of Northern Ireland, Scotland and Wales. Since 1997 there has been a restructuring of powers and responsibilities within the UK. There have been moves towards greater devolution, attempts at regional government and various strategies to invigorate local government. Changing attitudes have also influenced the way central government has organised and structured bodies like the NHS and the police (e.g. the introduction of directly elected Police Commissioners that mirror directly elected mayors).

Examiner tip

It is not necessary to understand what services each type of government delivers, but you do need to have an understanding that the different bodies have different powers and responsibilities. Studying the nearest type of authority to you, undertaking internet research or speaking to your local councillor is a good way of researching this topic.

It is very helpful if you can research local examples of levels of government and are able to quote them in your responses. The use of examples helps to increase your understanding. This website contains details of the work of all types of local authority: www.local.gov.uk

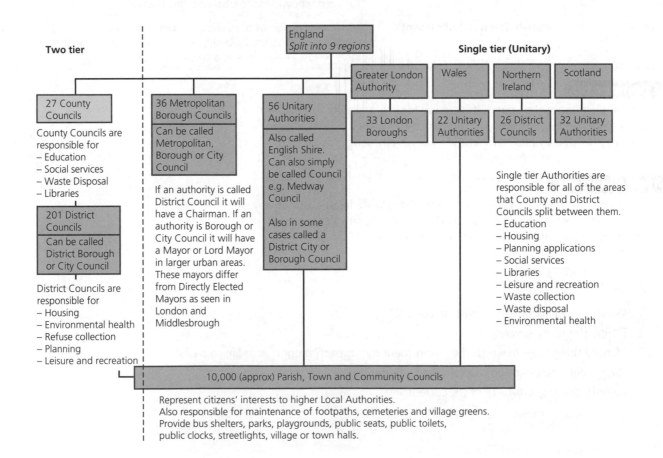

Two tier

England
Split into 9 regions

Single tier (Unitary)

Greater London Authority

Wales

Northern Ireland

Scotland

27 County Councils

36 Metropolitan Borough Councils

56 Unitary Authorities

33 London Boroughs

22 Unitary Authorities

26 District Councils

32 Unitary Authorities

County Councils are responsible for
– Education
– Social services
– Waste Disposal
– Libraries

Can be called Metropolitan, Borough or City Council

Also called English Shire. Can also simply be called Council e.g. Medway Council

201 District Councils

Can be called District Borough or City Council

If an authority is called District Council it will have a Chairman. If an authority is Borough or City Council it will have a Mayor or Lord Mayor in larger urban areas. These mayors differ from Directly Elected Mayors as seen in London and Middlesbrough

Also in some cases called a District City or Borough Council

District Councils are responsible for
– Housing
– Environmental health
– Refuse collection
– Planning
– Leisure and recreation

Single tier Authorities are responsible for all of the areas that County and District Councils split between them.
– Education
– Housing
– Planning applications
– Social services
– Libraries
– Leisure and recreation
– Waste collection
– Waste disposal
– Environmental health

10,000 (approx) Parish, Town and Community Councils

Represent citizens' interests to higher Local Authorities.
Also responsible for maintenance of footpaths, cemeteries and village greens.
Provide bus shelters, parks, playgrounds, public seats, public toilets, public clocks, streetlights, village or town halls.

The relationship between the centre and the locality

Two terms relate to this concept:

- **Devolve or devolution**: transfer of power and authority from a greater to a lesser body, i.e. Westminister to Scotland, or Westminister to local councils.
- *Ultra vires*: to act beyond your powers. If, for example, a council acts beyond its powers, individual councillors can be held to account.

The relationship between central and local government is based upon the principle that ultimate power resides with central government. No devolved body, regional or local government bodies can act outside the powers granted to it by Parliament.

Central government can, at any time, restructure, change the powers or dissolve other government bodies without any redress by local government. For example, the Greater London Council (GLC) was abolished in 1986 and wasn't replaced with the Greater London Authority (GLA) until 2000.

Central government controls, to a large extent, the expenditure of local and devolved government via both legislation and the amount of the central government grants they are awarded.

Devolution

The devolution of power to Scotland, Wales and Northern Ireland allowed these nations to make more decisions about the services provided in their own countries. The greatest powers were granted to Scotland which has its own Parliament. As well as being able to pass laws, it also has some tax varying powers. A recent issue regarding the centre/local relationship is the wish of a section of the Scottish population to gain either greater devolution (devomax) or full independence. It is likely that a referendum on this issue will be held before 2015.

Central and unitary authorities

The GLA was created after a previous government had dissolved the former central authority for London. The GLA is now headed by a directly elected mayor, another innovation which central government believes will increase public interest in local democracy and achieve greater accountability. In 2012, central government wished to create more directly elected mayors but they were turned down in 9 of the 11 areas where referendums took place.

Recent governments have also wished to increase the number of unitary authorities, a council that runs all the services in a given area. In Cornwall, for example, there is now only one council instead of the previous County and District council structure.

Websites

The Department for Communities and Local Government – this link relates to local government finance
www.communities.gov.uk/localgovernment/localgovernmentfinance
Comment on the referendums held regarding directly elected mayors May 2012:
www.bbc.co.uk/news/uk-politics-17949950

Chapter 10 The citizen and political power in the United Kingdom

Citizen participation in local government and the role of the elected representative

Revised

Citizen participation

- The involvement of the citizen is at the heart of the concept of local government.
- Citizens participate in the process as electors, giving local government a mandate and legitimacy.
- Local citizens can stand for election to local authorities and by becoming local councillors provide an accountability back to their local communities and represent the needs of their local community.
- Many local authorities encourage local participation through forums and formal consultation processes.
- Many councils organise Youth Councils where local young people can hold meetings that mirror their work.
- Planning issues often take the form of wide public consultations.

Role of the elected representative

- In the UK, councillors are representatives not delegates.
- They are free to vote according to their own wishes and are held accountable by their constituents at elections.
- Most councillors in the UK are nominated by political parties and form groups when elected, seeking to run the council as a majority group.
- Many councils in the UK are run by formal and informal coalitions where two or more parties work together.
- Like national government elections, local parties run for election on a party manifesto.
- Increasingly, local elections are seen as a barometer of national politics and often as an endorsement or warning to central government.
- Traditionally local councillors were unpaid volunteers, but today councillors receive allowances and major post-holders receive a salary that can vary from a few thousand to tens of thousands of pounds per year.

Local referendums

It is now possible for local citizens to set in motion a local referendum on a local topic. The government has also said that if a council wishes to increase local council tax beyond a set figure, they can only do so after a local referendum has been held.

Politicians of all parties are concerned about increasing voter apathy (see page 88) especially in regard to local government. Through directly elected mayors, formal consultations, giving more powers back to local councils and local referendums, parties hope to encourage more local citizens to take an interest and take part in local democracy.

Websites

The Joseph Rowntree Foundation research paper regarding citizen's involvement in local government (2009): www.jrf.org.uk/system/files/citizen-involvement-governance-summary.pdf

This government website allows you to research your own local council as well as giving an overview of local government in the UK: www.direct.gov.uk/en/governmentcitizensandrights/ukgovernment/localgovernment/dg_073310

Information about local referendums: www.iniref.org/local-referendum.html

Examiner tip

You don't need an in-depth knowledge of local government, but you need to understand the broad concepts within which local government operates, how citizens are involved in the process of local government, and what is currently being done to encourage greater interest and participation in local democracy.

Some knowledge of how local government operates within your area, and knowledge of local case studies, will add depth to your understanding.

Now test yourself

1 Identify two types of local authority that exist in England.
2 Identify three types of elected posts in the UK.
3 How is a unitary authority different from other local authorities?
4 What is the term used to describe an action taken by a council outside its powers?
5 Identify two ways in which most local citizens can take part in local democracy.

Answers on p.110

Tested

10.3 What is the impact of the EU on life in the UK?

Impact of the EU on the daily lives of citizens of the UK

Revised

In 1973, the UK became a member of the European Economic Community (EEC), which is now known as the European Union (EU). Since then, the actions of the EU have impacted on the daily lives of UK citizens.

- For many who oppose the UK's membership, this impact is seen as negative, intrusive and eroding UK sovereignty.
- For others, the impact is seen as raising or underpinning standards, and a price that one has to pay when becoming a member of a club that has certain common rules.

If you are an EU citizen:

- you have the right to travel, work and live anywhere in the EU
- if you have completed a university course lasting more than three years, your qualification will be recognised in all EU countries
- you can obtain an EU Health Insurance Card that provides health cover within the EU
- you have the right to vote or stand as a candidate in most elections in EU member states.

The EU:

- introduced a charter for air passengers that provides for refunds
- allows EU citizens to move around the EU without passport checks
- introduced regulations on mobile phone roaming charges and MP3 download charges
- has EU bathing water directives that safeguard the quality of UK beaches and bathing waters
- has a European Arrest Warrant which allows for the movement for those accused of a crime from one country to another within the EU.

> **Websites**
>
> Official EU website regarding benefits of membership to UK citizens: http://ec.europa.eu/unitedkingdom/pdf/the_eu_for_me_web.pdf

> **Examiner tip**
>
> This section of the course requires that you have an understanding of the impact of the EU rather than detailed knowledge, e.g. you need to know that some areas of life are impacted by the EU, while in other areas decisions are left to individual nation states.

The UK's relationship with Europe since the founding of the EEC

Revised

The relationship of the UK to Europe can be looked at as an ever-changing time line.

The views of the UK political parties when the EEC was set up

- When the original six member governments formed the EEC and held their meetings, the UK was invited to attend but only sent civil servants.
- The attitude of both the Conservative Party and the Labour Party was largely hostile to UK membership of the EU believing either that the UK's role in the world and its relationship with USA and the Commonwealth meant we had little to gain from joining any group, or were hostile

because they believed it was a capitalist club and that ordinary people would gain little from the UK's membership. Within both parties, there were also elements that did support EU membership.

- The then Liberal Party was the only party that was committed to the UK membership of the EU and at that time they were a very minor parliamentary party.

UK and EEC Timeline

1957	The six founding members France, Germany, Italy, Belgium, Netherlands and Luxembourg signed the Treaty Of Rome establishing the European Economic Community (EEC).
1959	The UK and other European countries formed the European Free Trade Association (EFTA). The other countries were Denmark, Austria, Norway, Portugal, Ireland, Sweden and Switzerland.
1961	The Conservative government applied to join the EEC but in 1963 the French government vetoed UK entry.
1967	The Labour government applied to join the EEC but again the French government vetoed UK membership.
1973	The Conservative government succeeded in negotiating UK membership of the EEC. The decision to join was taken after a vote in Parliament.
1975	The Labour government re-negotiated the terms of the UK's membership of the EEC and held a referendum to seek the public's support for the new agreement. The referendum resulted in 2:1 vote in favour of the new terms.

The Thatcher Years 1979–90

The Conservative government wished to achieve a rebate on the monies the UK contributed to the European Community (EC), and wanted to change the Common Agriculture Policy (CAP). In 1986, it wanted to push ahead with the Single Market Agreement, which it believed would assist the UK, particularly when the financial and service sectors across Europe operated to the same standards.

European splits in the Labour and Conservative parties

In 1983, Labour campaigned for the UK to leave the EEC. The Labour Party split in the early 1980s: the Social Democratic Party (SDP) was formed and joined an alliance with the Liberals and fought the 1983 and 1987 General Elections as an Alliance. The SDP later merged with the Liberals to form the present Liberal Democrats.

In 1992, the debate surrounding the Maastricht Treaty opened divides within the Conservative Party in government under John Major. The Treaty only passed in the House of Commons due to the support of the Liberals; a number of Conservative MPs voted against their own government. John Major negotiated a number of opt-outs for the UK regarding some policy areas and helped to develop the concept of 'subsidiarity', which means that any policy should be carried at the appropriate level of government, i.e. that member states determine what should be done by the EU. In September 1992 the UK was forced out of the European Exchange Rate Mechanism (ERM) by the financial markets. This system was a precursor to the current Euro currency.

New Labour and Europe 1997–2010

During the years of Labour government there was a desire to be at the heart of Europe, and initially one of the opt-outs became a part of UK law, the Social Chapter of the Maastricht Treaty. As the EU developed its own monetary system, the Euro, the UK government decided not to join.

In 1995 the UK government opted out of the Schengen Agreement, which allowed for the free flow of people from within the EU and the elimination of border controls.

> **Examiner tip**
>
> You are not expected to know about very twist and turn in regard to the UK attitudes to Europe, only to appreciate that they have changed over time and that the evolving nature of the EU causes major political issues in the UK.

Throughout this period both the Conservative and Labour parties supported the EU becoming a broader-based body by increasing its membership. It was believed that by encouraging new members especially those from behind the former Iron Curtain the moves towards greater integration and transfer of powers to the EU could be slowed down or reversed. The shorthand for this policy was 'breadth against depth'. There are currently 27 members states of the EU.

Typical mistake

Typical errors in questions relating to the EU are that the examples used are very dated. Make sure that you use contemporary examples to support the points you wish to make.

The impact upon the UK of EU membership

Revised

By joining the EEC in 1973, the UK agreed to pool and share elements of sovereignty. This arrangement only relates to areas of competence, which are agreed areas of policy where the EU can pass laws and issue directives. For example, the EU might intervene if the UK tries to amend its competition policy but it can have no say over the income rates applied to UK citizens.

Websites

The Charter of Fundamental Human Rights: http://europa.eu/legislation_summaries/justice_freedom_security/combating_discrimination/l33501_en.htm
The UK and the Single Market: a BIS Paper: www.bis.gov.uk/assets/biscore/international-trade-investment-and-development/docs/u/11-719-uk-and-single-market

- Impact of EU membership on political parties in the UK.
- The Conservative Party are 'Eurosceptics' which impinges on the position any Conservative Prime Minister can take.
- The Labour Party and the Liberal Democrats are pro-EU, although they do not promote this policy prominently due to negative portrayal in the media.
- The United Kingdom Independence Party (UKIP) was formed because it wanted the UK to withdraw from the EU. It has some success in elections.
- Because of the success of UKIP, there has been a call for a referendum on the UK membership of the EU.

All UK parties stand for election to the European Parliament and belong to transnational groupings in the Parliament. The Labour Party belongs to the Socialist Group (S&D), the Liberal Democrats belong to the Group of Alliance of Liberals and Democrats for Europe (ALDE) and the Conservative Party, which did belong to the largest group in the Parliament, the EPP, have now set up their own group with others called the European Conservatives and Reformist Group (ECR).

Impact of EU membership on UK law

By joining the EEC, the UK agreed that European law would have a higher status than UK law. The law determined by the EU always supersedes national law. Any conflict would ultimately be resolved by the European Court of Justice (the Court of the EU) and their decisions are binding on member countries.

As a part of the Maastricht Treaty, there was a Social Chapter outlining workers' and others' rights. This was initially subject to a UK opt-out, but in 1997 the Labour government reversed the policy so that the rights of UK workers regarding maternity and paternity leave and the rights of casual and part-time workers are the same as in other EU countries.

In 2000 the EU also developed the Charter of Fundamental Rights of the European Union which enshrined numerous human and social rights. The Charter came into force in 2009 when the Treaty of Lisbon was signed.

Impact of EU membership on UK economy

Economically the UK has always pushed for an open and free market within the EU. This was the reason for the UK's support for the Single Market Act in 1985.

The following is a quotation from the Department for Business Innovations and Skills (2012), regarding the role of trade with the EU:

The Single Market is vital to the UK's prosperity. It gives UK business access to the world's largest market with 500 million people generating about £10 trillion economic activity. European markets account for half of the UK's overall trade and foreign investments. As a result, around 3.5 million jobs in the UK are linked to the export of goods and services to the EU.

The Single Market has been a key driver for economic growth in the UK and in Europe. EU countries currently trade twice as much with each other as they would do in the absence of the Single Market. As a result, the Single Market may be responsible for income gains in the UK between 2 per cent and 6 per cent, that is between £1100 and £3300 a year per British household.

The contrasting workings of 'government' of the UK and the EU

Revised

The workings of the UK government

- The UK is a constitutional monarchy where the monarch has handed over almost all of their powers to government. The monarch still has to give the Royal Assent to laws before they are passed, but no recent monarch by convention has refused to sign.

- Governments are normally formed after a general election. Every constituency (seat) elects one Member of Parliament (MP), and the party with a majority of the seats is asked by the monarch to form a government. If no party has a majority, as in 2010, a coalition can be formed of more than one party.

- All government ministers are Members of Parliament. Parliament discusses and passes all legislation.

- The civil service in the UK is a permanent body that is politically neutral.

The workings of the EU government

- The EU is both a **supranational** body, where powers have been granted to it by its members, and an **intergovernmental** body, where decisions are made by the member states.

- The last major reform of the workings of the EU took place in 2009 with the Treaty of Lisbon.

The EU is organised around three major bodies:

The Parliament

- The Parliament is directly elected by the citizens of the EU, which over the years has seen its powers increase.

> **Websites**
>
> The website of the President of the European Council: www.european-council.europa.eu/the-president

> **Intergovernmental** – a process of decision making, within an internal organisation, in which all national governments meet and have equal influence.

- It has the power of co-decision with the Council and this impacts upon 95 per cent of all legislation. If both sides cannot agree the matter goes before a conciliation committee.
- Secondly they have the power to give assent to all EU international treaties negotiated by the Commission.
- The Parliament also shares responsibility with the Council for agreeing the budget of the EU.
- The Parliament also has the power to accept or reject Commissioner members.

The Commission

- The Commission is made up of political appointees from the member countries and, under the President of the Commission, they are given roles similar in a way to UK government ministers.
- The Commission is supported in their work by civil servants seconded from member states.
- The Commission generates the ideas for new policies, which it sends to the Council and the Parliament.

The Council

- The Council of Ministers known as the Council is made up of ministers from the member states who meet by policy area, i.e. all the transport ministers meet together.
- The Council is headed by a different member state every six months, which is able to set the agenda for their six months in office.
- The European Council is the EU's top political body. It consists of the member countries' Heads of State or Government. It normally meets four times a year. It has a permanent President who co-ordinates the work of the European Council. The current post-holder is Herman van Rompuy, a former Prime Minister of Belgium.

Examiner tip

You only need to know the key aspects of how these bodies work and their inter-relationship.

Now test yourself

Tested ☐

1. When did the UK join the EEC?
2. Why was the Maastricht Treaty important?
3. To which political groups in the European Parliament do the three major parties in the UK belong?
4. What does the term 'intergovernmental' mean?
5. Which body within the EU has gained increasing powers over the years?

Answers on p.110

Exam practice

'The UK government provides too many services to its citizens'. Present a case for or against this point of view.   **(15 marks)**

Answers and quick quiz online

Online ☐

Examiner tip

Often questions are posed to provoke a broad response enabling you to show your understanding of a specific concept. In the case of this exemplar question: What is the role of the state? Should it provide more or fewer services to its citizens?

You need to have some understanding of what the state currently provides but it is not necessary to got into lots of detail. The core issue is whether you can make an argument for or against the proposition. Make your case point by point and support your views with evidence. There is no correct answer to this type of question – either point of view, if well argued, can gain full marks.

Chapter 11 Playing your part: how the citizen can get involved and make a difference

11.1 What does 'taking part in the democratic process' mean?

The concept of democracy

Democracy	• An overarching term that describes a system of government which is based on the principle that ultimate power belongs to the citizens of the state who make decisions about the future of the state.
	• Countries and governmental systems that call themselves democratic interpret the term differently, so no state has a system that meets the pure definition.
Direct democracy	• This is where decisions are made by the people and not through representatives or delegates.
	• This is the purest form of democracy, but outside of small communities it is impractical for everyone in the state to meet to debate and vote on every issue.
	• Referendums are forms of direct democracy as citizens are involved in the decision making by voting on a single issue.
	• Modern technology allows more people to become involved in making decisions, but there is reluctance by political parties in the UK to move too quickly down this route.
Indirect democracy/ Representative democracy	• These two terms are interchangeable. They mean a system of government that relies upon representatives of the people making decisions on their behalf.
	• In most systems this is achieved through the electoral system. A representative is someone elected who is free to vote on issues as they see fit. The electorate has the ability to decide their future at the next election. A delegate is an appointed or elected person who has to vote according to the instruction of the people they represent.
	• The UK has always had a system of representative democracy and this developed into a system of party politics whereby most of those elected at all levels in the UK belong to and are sponsored by a political party. There are current proposals that citizens in the UK should be able to hold a recall election to hold their MP to account between general elections.
Liberal democracy	• This is a form of representative democracy.
	• There are regular and free elections.
	• The political system involves competing political parties and contains a range of pressure and interest groups. (This is a definition also of a pluralist system.)
	• The power of those elected are defined by law or a formal constitution.
	• The rights of the citizen are defined and safeguarded by an independent judiciary.

> **Examiner tip**
>
> You need to have an understanding of these key concepts and be able to support your understanding with examples and any recent events that relate to the concept.

Democratic values: rights, freedoms, equality
Revised

Democratic values

- The concept of democracy is based upon a political system that holds certain values.

- Many values, while retaining the same language, have developed and evolved and continue to evolve, for example who is entitled to vote. Originally it was only some men who owned property, now it is an all-encompassing term, but there is still a contemporary debate about the rights of sixteen-year-olds and those of prisoners.

- Other values associated with democracy are:
  - freedom of speech, both for individuals and the media
  - freedom of assembly, to be able to gather together or meet others
  - the rule of law where no one is above the law and the law treats everyone equally.

Rights, freedoms, equality

Rights, freedoms and equality underpin our democratic system. Most are now enshrined in legislation that protects individual citizens and limits the power of government, e.g. the Human Rights Act 1998.

How democratic is the UK?

There is no correct conclusion to the question 'How democratic is the UK?' as many of the issues relate to a citizen's own viewpoint.

The UK is very democratic	The UK is not very democratic
All citizens can vote.	You must be registered to vote; only those over eighteen can vote; prisoners in the UK cannot vote.
Anyone over eighteen can stand for election.	It is very difficult for an independent to get elected; the party system is very strong.
The UK has a stable government, which represents the people.	No UK government since 1935 has been elected by over 50 per cent of the electorate.
The UK has a free press.	It is very difficult for a citizen to seek redress against the media.
All citizens have access to the legal system.	The legal system is complex and very expensive.
The government has introduced **e-petitioning** to allow the public concerns to be heard.	Whether a debate takes place after e-petitioning is still decided by politicians.

> **Websites**
>
> The United Nations Declaration of Human Rights: www.un.org/en/documents/udhr
> Council of Europe – Convention on Human Rights: www.echr.coe.int/nr/rdonlyres/d5cc24a7-dc13-4318-b457-5c9014916d7a/0/englishanglais.pdf
> Human rights Act 1998: www.equalityhumanrights.com/human-rights/what-are-human-rights/the-human-rights-act

E-petition – The UK government has set up an e-petition website where members of the public can start an online petition. If 100,000 people sign the petition, it is referred to a House of Commons committee which decides whether it should be discussed in the House of Commons.

> **Examiner tip**
>
> Think about which points in the table are strongest to help you make your own judgement as to how democratic the UK is.

Opportunities and barriers to citizen participation

Citizens in the UK traditionally participate in the democratic process via the ballot box, exercising their vote at an election.

Since the 1950s, there has been a decline in voter participation. During the same period there has also been a decline in the individual membership of political parties. This in itself leads to a smaller group of voluntary workers for political parties, and a smaller number from which they can select to contest elections on behalf of the parties.

Some parties now have open hustings meetings where any member of the public can attend to select the candidate for the party. Others have tried to have women-only selections to encourage a better balance of elected representatives.

There has, however, been an increase in informal politics and single issue politics since the 1950s. More people than ever before now belong to pressure groups and interest groups. Some have a larger membership than that of all the political parties combined. Far more people are getting involved in issues related to their local area regarding the environment or transport.

The government has taken several initiatives to encourage civic participation:

- e-petitioning of Parliament
- the Localism Bill giving local authorities more powers
- establishing directly elected Police Commissioners
- organising referendums on directly elected mayors.

Now test yourself

1 Give a brief definition of democracy.
2 What is the difference between direct and indirect democracy?
3 Give one reason why you believe the UK is a democratic country.
4 How are citizens increasingly getting involved in the political process?
5 What is e-petitioning?

Answers on p.110

11.2 Citizens and the electoral process

Knowledge of the electoral process

Traditionally the UK electoral process is associated with the First Past the Post (FPTP) electoral system, whereby the candidate with the most votes wins and if more than one candidate needs to be elected, the next candidates in order are elected. Since the introduction of directly elected Members of the European Parliament (MEPs), the number of electoral systems used in the UK has increased. Since 1979, the Northern Ireland members of the European Parliament have been elected using the Single Transferrable Vote (STV), a proportional system.

Websites

The Electoral Commission, the official body that oversees all electoral matters in the UK: www.electoralcommission.org.uk
The Electoral Reform Society where details can be found of how the various systems operate: www.electoral-reform.org.uk

The differing systems used in the UK

Voting system	Description	Advantages	Disadvantages
CLOSED PARTY LIST, e.g. European Parliament	Voters cast a single vote X for a party on a party list. The number of votes gained by the party determines how many of their members are elected.	This system lends itself to greater proportionality than others.	The voter has no choice regarding the order of the candidates on the party list.
FIRST PAST THE POST (FPTP) **UK Parliament**	The candidate with most votes wins. A non-proportional system. A referendum was held in May 2012 to change the way we elect Members of Parliament to the AV system. The proposal was rejected.	This is a simple to use system. The outcome is known quickly.	People can be elected on a minority of the vote. Governments are elected on a minority of the vote. Smaller parties are under represented.
Local Authority elections in England and Wales	Councils can choose to call an election every three years, or a third to retire each year. County councillors are elected every four years.		
SINGLE TRANSFERRABLE VOTE (STV) e.g. **European Parliament (Northern Ireland)** **Northern Ireland Assembly** **Northern Ireland Local Councils** **Scottish Local Councils**	Proportional system where the electors place candidates in number order. Each candidate must achieve a quota of votes to win. Votes above the quota are redistributed to the voters' lower choices.	Every vote does help elect someone. The result closely matches the vote cast for each party.	This system often leads to many parties electing candidates. Coalition governments are more likely. Results can take time to count.
SUPPLEMENTARY VOTE (SV) **Directly elected Mayors** **Police Commisioners**	Voters have a first and second choice candidate. The winner must receive over 50 per cent of the votes. Lowest scoring candidates are elected and their second votes redistributed.	Ensures that the winner has over 50 per cent of the vote cast.	Often the winner relies on others' second choices.
ADDITIONAL MEMBER SYSTEM (AMS) **Scottish Parliament** **Welsh Assembly** **Greater London Authority**	Voters have two votes, one for a candidate and the second for a party list. The first votes operate as a FPTP system and the second act as a top-up vote to ensure that the overall vote is proportional when additional members are elected from the party list.	Ensures that the wishes of the voters are more closely aligned to the outcome.	Ends up with two types of elected member. One directly elected and another from a list.

> **Examiner tip**
>
> You are expected to know how and where the various systems operate, whether they are proportional or majority systems and the impact the system has on the outcome of elections and government formation; also the main point made in their favour and against their use.

Unit 2 Democracy, Active Citizenship and Participation

Who can vote?	In the UK you can register to vote if you are over sixteen, and a British or Irish citizen, or a qualifying Commonwealth or EU citizen who is resident in the UK. You can only exercise your vote when you reach the age of eighteen. Citizens of the EU who are not Commonwealth citizens or citizens of the Republic of Ireland can vote in European and local elections in the UK, but are not able to vote in UK parliamentary general elections or referendums.
Who can stand for election?	You can stand as a candidate in the general election, Scottish Parliament, Welsh and Northern Ireland Assembly if you are eighteen years old or over, and either a British citizen, a citizen of the Republic of Ireland, or a citizen of some Commonwealth countries. Certain people may not stand for election, such as members of the police forces, members of the armed forces, serving civil servants or judges, certain convicted prisoners or those declared bankrupt. To stand in a local election you must be a registered local government elector in the local authority areas, both on the day you are nominated and Election Day; or have lived or worked, or occupied land or premises in the local authority area for twelve months prior to the election.
Who can stand as a Police Commissioner?	• You must be eighteen or older as per parliamentary requirements. • You must not have been convicted of an imprisonable offence. You cannot be a serving: • civil servant • judge • police officer • member of the regular armed forces • employee of a council within the force area • employee of a police-related agency • employee of another government agency • politically restricted post-holder • member of police staff (including PCSOs) • member of a police authority • MEPs, MSPs, AMs and MPs will be able to stand as PCCs, but will need to stand down from their existing post before being able to accept the post of PCC.

Electoral participation: turnout patterns and voter apathy

• Voter turnout relates to the number of voters who actually turn out and vote compared against the number of electors on the electoral register.

• Voter apathy relates to voters not wishing to take part in the electoral process and showing a disinterest in politics.

The turnout in recent general elections has increased:

• In the 1950s the figure was over 70 per cent.

• In 2001 it was 59.1 per cent.

• In 2005 it was 61.3 per cent.

• In 2010 it was 65.1 per cent.

The pattern of social class voting indicates that the higher the social class the more likely you are to vote. In the 2010 General Election 76 per cent of professional people voted whilst only 57 per cent of people from a poorer background did so.

Websites

The Hansard Society produces a series of papers about political participation: http://hansardsociety. org.uk/blogs/parliament_and_ government/pages/audit-of-political-engagement.aspx

Election campaigning and its impact on citizens

- Election campaigns traditionally take place in the UK around three to five weeks before the election date.

- There are clear legal requirements regarding how much candidates can spend on their election, but there is no limit upon the money a party can spend to promote its policies.

- There are no limits on what other organisations can spend to promote ideas during an election and these ideas often relate to the policies of a particular political party.

- Traditionally in the UK candidates held local meetings where voters could question the candidates. Today very few local meetings are held. Meetings are only arranged when a major party figure attends and often these are closed meetings that are only open to party supporters.

- Parties at a General Election have the facility of Party Political Broadcasts on radio and television. This service is provided free of charge.

- Parties invest in poster board campaigns and newspaper advertising.

- Every candidate publishes their own leaflets and during a general election, candidates are entitled to have leaflets delivered free of charge by the Royal Mail.

- Newspapers and other media are able to support the party of their own choice and it has been traditionally thought that newspaper endorsement helped parties win elections.

- During the 2010 General Election, the first three leader debates took place and millions of viewers were able to become informed and follow the debate.

- Increasingly political parties are using new media to help them campaign: running internet sites, using Twitter and Facebook, and using e-mail to canvas as well as the telephone.

The extent to which campaigns make an impact on voting intentions is contested. The Liberal Democrats have traditionally increased their vote during a campaign, but this may be due to their greater media coverage rather than their campaign. During the televised leaders' debates of 2010, the Liberal Democrat leader Nick Clegg appeared to score well in opinion polls after the debates. However, the party's votes and seats declined when the election results came in.

> **Websites**
>
> The Guardian article below is about the links to policy and the campaign outcomes in the 2010 General Election: www.guardian.co.uk/news/datablog/2010/may/04/general-election-2010-data

Chapter 11 Playing your part: how the citizen can get involved and make a difference

Role of the media, opinion polling and focus groups in forming political opinions

Opinion polling: Public opinion relates to the beliefs and attitudes that people have regarding issues, events or personalities. One means of collecting this information is opinion polling which can take a variety of forms: written; telephone interviews; online questioning; focus groups. Most opinion polling in the UK is undertaken by professional polling organisations that have a range of customers from commercial companies to political parties and pressure and interest groups.

Focus groups: Increasingly, political parties wish to tailor their message to the needs of the electors they need to attract. Many use focus groups where a cross-section of people are questioned together to ascertain their attitude to certain prompts and statements.

Traditionally, a citizen's voting intentions were governed by social class, education, employment, religion and regional identity. Today the electorate appears more fluid and willing to switch who they vote for from one election to another.

The media: The role of the media has always seemed important in forming political attitudes, as they were the means by which the citizen obtained their information. The growth of the internet has allowed citizens to have a greater range of sources of information and views.

Commercial media can set an agenda that can in turn impact on political attitudes. Many citizens who buy commercial media often make their choice based on the views that they believe that media to have, for example, a Conservative inclined reader is more likely to read the *Daily Telegraph* than the *Guardian*.

Websites

Ipsos/Mori Polling organization:
www.ipsos-mori.com
Yougov polling organization:
http://yougov.co.uk

Now test yourself

1 Identify one benefit of the FPTP electoral system.
2 What system is used to elect members to the Scottish Parliament?
3 What do you understand by the term 'electoral turnout'?
4 What is a focus group?
5 What system is being used to elect Police Commissioners?

Answers on pp.110–111

11.3 Do pressure groups improve the democratic process?

What is a pressure group?

A pressure group is a group of citizens who seek to influence those who make decisions to secure the interests or views of their supporters. These groups can be local, national or international. They can have a few members or millions of members.

Examples of pressure groups

RSPCA	Animal Liberation Front	Britain in Europe	European Movement
Confederation of British Industry	Countryside Alliance	Welsh Language Society	Greenpeace
Friends of the Earth	Surfers Against Sewage	Rowers Against Thames Sewage (RATS)	Fathers4Justice
Mothers Apart from their Children	NSPCC	Campaign for Real Ale	Amnesty International
Liberty	Christian Aid	Oxfam	Charter88
Electoral Reform Society	Migration Watch UK	Muslim Council of Britain	Taxpayers Alliance
British Humanist Association	Fawcett Society	Electoral Reform Society	FOREST

These examples give an indication of the range of issues where citizens work together to bring about change.

Types of pressure groups: insider/outsider Revised

- Not all pressure groups operate in the same ways. Pressure groups are classified in different ways by their status, the nature of the issue they are concerned about and by the methods they use.
- **Single cause groups:** These pressure groups focus on a single issue, e.g. those opposed to the (HS2) high speed train development.
- **Multi cause groups:** These are groups that seek to influence policy and decisions over a range of issues, such as trade unions that seek to influence policy on pay, hours, health and safety, pensions, discrimination, etc., e.g. The National Union of Rail, Maritime and Transport Workers (RMT).
- **Protective:** groups that seek to protect the interests of their members, for example the British Medical Association which is the professional body that speaks on behalf of doctors
- **Promotional:** these are groups that wish to promote an issue to their members and other interested parties on a particular topic, e.g. Greenpeace is interested in environmental issues.

Groups are also classified as to their status as insider or outsider groups.

Insider status implies that the group is able to discuss, meet with and is consulted by those it wishes to influence. For example, if there were changes to rural planning regulations the government would consult the Campaign for Rural England (CPRE) but would be unlikely to involve the Countryside Alliance which is seen as an outsider group in direct talks or negotiations.

Outsider status are groups that do not have direct access to those making decisions and are not consulted or directly involved in discussions. These groups often seek outsider status, not wishing to be a part of the 'system' of talks and negotiations. They are often deemed to be outsiders because the methods they use often involving direct action. Fathers4Justice would be labelled as an outsider group.

> **Websites**
>
> **Pressure group opposing the HS2 High Speed Rail Link:** http://stophs2.org
> **Transport Union:** www.rmt.org.uk
> **British Medical Association:** http://bma.org.uk
> **Greenpeace:** www.greenpeace.org.uk
> **Campaign to Protect Rural England:** www.cpre.org.uk
> **Countryside Alliance:** www.countryside-alliance.org/ca
> **Fathers 4 Justice:** www.fathers-4-justice.org

The targets and tactics of pressure groups

Direct action	When individuals or groups take action to highlight an issue. These activities can be violent or non-violent and can target individuals, groups or institutions. Examples: strikes, occupations; civil disobedience, protests, boycotts, marches and demonstrations. Recent examples include the trade union protests against public sector pension changes, students protesting against the ending of EMA and increase in university tuition fees.
Illegal direct action	Acts which break the law. Examples: acts of terrorism, violence, bombing, criminal damage to property, releasing animals into the wild, occupying property.
Protest	This can take many forms, for example marches and demonstrations, parading with placards, standing outside and blockading a business.
Lobbying	This involves pressure group members meeting those they wish to influence. An example of a direct form of action is meeting MPs in the Lobby of the House of Commons, or meeting their local councillors.
	An example of indirect action is writing letters or e-mails.
Boycotts	Where individuals try to convince others not to purchase goods or services from an institution because they disagree with the policy of that organisation. A successful boycott may target linked organisations to stop them supplying or purchasing from a named company.
Civil disobedience	Where individuals or groups refuse to undertake actions, i.e. paying a tax demand or refusing to vote or register. The phrase is associated with the teaching of Mahatma Gandhi and his protests to gain Indian independence from the British when he led mass non-violent civil disobedience campaigns. When a new local tax was introduced in Scotland, one act of civil disobedience was for people not to register on the voters or poll tax registers so they couldn't be traced.
Indirect action	This is supporting a cause without taking direct action.
Publicity	Displaying information or support for the group, for example on a poster or car sticker.
Leaflet and advertisements	Assisting in writing, publishing or delivering leaflets.
Petitions	Signing a petition to show your support for a cause.
Providing research	Providing information or replying to a survey by a group expressing your support.

Pressure groups and the influence of the citizen

There are a range of views on the topic of pressure groups and the influence of the citizen, and there is no clear-cut answer. You must use the evidence and arrive at your own conclusion. Here are some of the points you need to bear in mind when arriving at your judgement.

Websites

A list of successful boycotts: www.ethicalconsumer.org/linkclick.aspx?fileticket=cOrT55txMvl%3D

This article outlines the work of the leading 12 UK Think Tanks: www.telegraph.co.uk/news/politics/1576447/The-top-twelve-think-tanks-in-Britain.html

A leading Lobbying group, Political Lobbying and Media Relations: www.plmr.co.uk

Points that support the view that pressure groups strengthen the influence of the citizen	Points that do not support the view that pressure groups strengthen the influence of the citizen
More people belong to pressure groups than political parties.	Pressure groups have too much influence, as they are concerned about a narrow issue.
Pressure groups speak up for the public on issues that politicians don't discuss.	Politicians pay too much attention to pressure groups all of whom are unrepresentative groups.
Pressure groups exert pressure on issues between elections.	Pressure groups are themselves undemocratic and often use non-democratic methods.
If pressure groups did not exist, politicians could ignore a large number of issues.	Some insider groups exert too much power and influence to the detriment of the whole population.
Pressure groups can raise immediate issues with politicians.	Politicians are too concerned with immediate headlines and over-react to every protest.

When thinking about pressure groups, you should also consider the role of think tanks and lobby groups.

Think tanks	Small groups that are privately funded to investigate a narrow range of issues.
	Many of these groups have a broad political agenda and wish to promote debate by producing research papers with recommendations. These groups are very influential in regard to the promotion of public policy and are used by political groups to promote new ideas to see how the public react.
Lobby groups	Commercial professional bodies that undertake work on behalf of their clients to promote the group's cause.
	They normally claim to have access to all levels of government, including European, and be able to access key decision makers. The government is currently drafting legislation regarding the registration of such organisations.

Examiner tip

The best way to revise this topic is through a range of case studies that demonstrate all the major elements of how pressure groups work, i.e. local, national, international, insider and outsider and other groups such as think tanks and lobby groups.

Now test yourself

Tested ☐

1 What is a pressure group?
2 What is an advantage of insider status?
3 What type of pressure group category would a trade union fall into into?
4 Identify an example of direct action.
5 What is a think tank?

Answers on p.111

Exam practice

Critically assess why some pressure groups in the UK are more influential than others.

(15 marks)

Answers and quick quiz online

Online ☐

Examiner tip

This question requires a short essay-style response. Ask yourself what is the core of the question – why some pressure groups are more influential than others. You clearly need to have some examples of more influential and less influential pressure groups. You need to define what influential means – achieving their aims. A well-structured response would:

1 Define influential.
2 Briefly quote some case studies of both extremes of influence.
3 Develop a series of points regarding their success relating the points back to your case studies: status, level of support, nature of the issue, media coverage, etc.

Typical mistake

Some students make the mistake of answering exam questions about pressure groups without mentioning any specific examples, using very dated examples or using examples that have no connection to the UK. Make sure you use up-to-date examples of pressure groups in the UK.

Chapter 12 Citizenship in action: citizens working together to bring about change

12.1 How do citizens bring about change?

The methods that campaigners use to bring about change

Traditionally members of the public would lobby officials or elected representatives. The term comes from the lobby of the House of Commons where the public is allowed to meet the Members of Parliament.

Other methods a campaigner might use:

- writing a letter of support for a campaign
- signing a petition to support a campaign
- donating money to support a campaign
- purchasing campaigning goods which both provides funds and publicity for the campaign
- organising a local or national march to demonstrate the level of support they have
- demonstrating at a set place to draw attention to their cause

- boycotting goods or services to bring attention to their cause
- attempting to influence the agenda by seeking media attention either through their actions or their research about an issue
- taking illegal action to promote their cause and thereby hope to attract media attention, i.e. occupying buildings. Some resort to violence or the threat of violence to organisations and individuals.

When considering each of these actions, think about the following questions:

- Are they likely to gain campaign members' support?
- Will they gain media attention?

- Will they promote a positive or negative image of the campaign?
- Will they improve the chances of achieving the aims of the campaign?

The role of new technologies in democratic participation and debates

New technologies enable protestors to ensure that their message is available to a large audience at a moment's notice. The development of the internet and social networking sites has enabled campaigns to become international very quickly. Not only can campaigners post their own version of events online, they can add pictures and video evidence and use their websites to encourage people to join or support them and fund them.

Governmental bodies are also aware of the benefits of the internet. Every government maintains websites, many of which are interactive. Most heads of government maintain websites and Twitter accounts so that people can follow what they are doing. Even Her Majesty the Queen maintains a Twitter site: @BritishMonarchy. The UK government has set up an e-petition site where members of the public can start an online petition: http://epetitions.direct.gov.uk. If 100,000 sign the petition, it is referred to a House of Commons committee which decides whether it should be discussed in the House of Commons.

UK-based case studies of campaigns to bring about change, led by citizens or groups (not political parties)

Revised

Jamie Oliver www.jamieoliver.com/jamies-ministry-of-food/	A well-known chef used a television series to campaign for an improvement in the quality of meals in UK schools. The support he achieved enabled him to pressure government to introduce changes. The campaign has now grown to involve the USA and improving the quality of food for all.
Hugh Fearnley-Whittingstall www.fishfight.net/hugh-fearnley-whittingstall/	Another chef who has campaigned successfully regarding changing EU fishing policy. He was concerned about the policy of throwing fish that had been caught back into the sea. The EU has now reviewed its policy due to his campaign, which went international following a series of television programmes.
Martha Payne	Martha Payne is a nine-years-old pupil in a Scottish Primary school who started a blog about her school dinners. The blog went viral and within a short period of time over 5,000,000 people had visited the site. The local council tried to stop Martha taking photos of her school dinners but due to public pressure they changed their mind. Martha started a campaign to raise money for charity from viewers of her blog. The Mary's Meals charity has raised over £80,000 as a result. A school kitchen is being built in Malawi with the money raised and is being named after Martha.

Successful and unsuccessful campaigns

Revised

For this topic, you will need to research some examples of successful and unsuccessful campaigns. As well as examples of national campaigns like the ones mentioned above, you need to find examples of local campaigns by looking on websites of local newspapers, radio and television, as well as the web pages of national campaigns to see if they have local groups running local campaigns.

Now test yourself

1 Identify one advantage of organising a march.
2 What media advantage did Jamie Oliver have over other campaigns?
3 How did Martha Payne's campaign become so well known?
4 Identify one advantage of using Twitter to campaign.

Answers on p.111

Tested

12.2 What are the key factors in successful campaigning?

The range of factors required for a successful campaign

Revised

Membership	Mass membership of a pressure group can be useful in gaining public support. However, it also can appear that a large group is acting in self-interest and therefore put the public off their cause. Small membership organisations like think tanks can often have influence well beyond their membership size. Some groups, especially professional groups like the BMA, can often achieve their objectives despite being relatively small in numbers. As was proved recently groups like the petrol tanker delivery drivers have immense power in that they can quickly bring society to a halt.
Finance	A well-financed campaign can often attract more attention than a poorly financed group. Raising large amounts of funds from large numbers of supporters can also enhance a cause. Funding helps groups to establish powerful media campaigns and even employ professional lobbyists. Even a small amount of funding can lead to an effective campaign, for example think tanks employ few people but through their networking and contacts can have immense influence.

The media	Media support can make or break campaigns. For example, Fathers4Justice were initially supported by the press and gained a lot of television coverage, but later the press turned against the campaign. The campaigns run by Jamie Oliver and Hugh Fearnley-Whittingstall would have gained little support if it were not for the television programmes they produced about the issues. In 1979 Roy Jenkins, the former deputy leader of the Labour Party, Chancellor of the Exchequer and President of the European Commission gave the annual televised Dimbleby Lecture on the BBC. As a result of the broadcast a new political party was formed, the Social Democratic Party (SDP).
Nature of the cause	Clearly the nature of a pressure group cause will impact on membership, finance and media support. A major non-controversial campaign like Jamie Oliver's School Dinner campaign is more likely to succeed as the cause is one with which no one could disagree. A campaign to abolish the monarchy may be popular with some but most of the population would be in disagreement and it would lack media support. Greenpeace often runs campaigns with which people agree and are prepared to use direct action methods, which bring their members into disputes with those they are contesting. This often causes issues with the media and government bodies.
Group status	Whether the group has insider or outsider status, and the methods they use, can impact upon the success of a pressure group. Greenpeace is an outsider group and is not involved by some governments in policy formation. An insider like the Law Society will be involved with the government in discussions about legal issues.
Methods	The range and type of methods used by a group can impact upon their success. The use of direct action methods whilst gaining media attention can alienate the group they wish to influence. Some methods involving mass support can achieve their ends. Others like the Countryside Alliance Rally and the Stop the War Coalition marches in London, despite involving thousands of people, did not achieve their aims. Sometimes indirect methods on local issues can be enough to achieve the aims of the group.

Why different factors can impact upon the success of a specific campaign

Revised ☐

The campaigns listed below have each developed differently due to different factors.

Group	Aim	Methods	Factors impacting upon success
Countryside Alliance	Pro-hunting and protecting rural life	Lobbying petitions and mass demonstrations and marches.	The campaign was perceived by the Labour government as being dominated by Conservative supporters and politically the issue was more important to the Conservatives than the Labour Party regarding potential electoral harm. The government therefore pursued its policy.
Jamie Oliver and School Dinners	Improve the quality of state school meals	Petitions and meetings with the Prime Minister and other government ministers	The campaign had mass success and could damage the Labour government so the government provided additional funds and established a food standards trust.
Fathers4Justice	Change the law regarding fathers' access to children following marriage breakdown	• Media attention stunts dressed up in costumes. • Staged sit-ins at ministers' homes, outside courts and on Buckingham Palace. • Throwing powder at the Prime Minister in the House of Commons.	The campaign gained a lot of media support and momentum, but by its actions the government were concerned if they appeared to agree to the campaigns wishes they would appear to be supporting the actions of the group. To date no major changes have taken place.
Stop the War Coalition	Stop the war in Iraq and Afghanistan	Lobbying, mass demonstrations and some encampments	Politically the Labour government supported both wars so therefore could not afford to appear to change its mind, as this would damage its political reputation. In the 1980s CND and other anti-nuclear weapon groups faced the same situation with the Conservative government which could not change its political position.

Exam practice answers and quick quizzes at **www.therevisionbutton.co.uk/myrevisionnotes**

Contemporary campaigning examples

Revised

In order to write about this topic it is important to follow current affairs and research contemporary campaigns. A useful website to use as a starting point is 38 degrees which acts as a website forum for numerous UK-based campaigns: www.38degrees.org.uk. Consider a range of campaigns: study a campaign being organised by a trade union, study an international campaign and consider an environmental campaign.

Now test yourself

Tested

1 What is an advantage of a pressure group having a large membership?
2 How can the media help a campaign?
3 How does insider status help a pressure group?
4 Identify one campaign and discuss why it was successful.
5 Why was the Stop the War campaign unsuccessful?

Answers on p.111

12.3 The impact of campaigns on political decision-making and political attitudes

Campaigns and their impact regarding bringing about change

Revised

By its nature, the study of citizenship deals with live and current issues, so when examples are used in the specification they are being used for illustrative purposes. When writing about campaigns, always attempt to write about contemporary UK-based campaigns. Examples from 2012 are: www.stopwar.org.uk, www.countryside-alliance.org/ca, www.fathers-4-justice.org.

In regards to each group/campaign you select you need to ask the following questions to arrive at a decision as to whether they are successful or not in bringing about change:

● What are they trying to achieve? What is their overall aim?
● For whom do they derive their support?
● What groups, bodies or institutions are they trying to influence?
● What methods are they using to achieve their aims?
● What degree of media support do they achieve?
● What is their status as a pressure group?
● To what extent have they achieved their aims?

Using this scaffold will help you assess the key elements of this part of the specification.

The impact of various campaigns on political decision-making and political attitudes

Whilst pressure groups are one source of campaign, other bodies also campaign to bring about change. The following are examples of other bodies which have campaigned for change.

The *Guardian* newspaper has led the campaign to get to the truth about telephone hacking. Its campaign eventually led to the establishment of the Leveson Inquiry regarding media ethics. See www.levesoninquiry.org.uk.

Kony 2012 is a short film produced by Invisible Children which was released on 5 March 2012. Its aim is to promote the charity Stop Kony, a movement that wishes to bring Joseph Kony before the International Criminal Court by December 2012. The campaign spread virally after being placed on the internet. Within weeks it had 86 million viewings. See www.kony2012.com

The Church of England took a stand against a government proposal to allow homosexual marriage. It has gathered a 500,000-signature petition and has launched a report giving its views. The Church of England would normally be seen very much as an insider group, but on this issue is using methods associated with traditional pressure groups: www.churchofengland. org/our-views/marriage,-family-and-sexuality-issues/same-sex-marriage.aspx

In order to make a judgement about the impact of any campaign you need to review its objectives against actions taken by those it wishes to influence.

- The *Guardian* campaign has been successful in that politicians have responded and established a public inquiry. The way the government acts upon the recommendation from the inquiry will determine whether or not the *Guardian* campaign was successful.

- The Kony campaign will be successful if Joseph Kony appears before the International Criminal Court.

- The Church of England campaign will be successful if no change is made to the current legislation relating to marriage.

Now test yourself

1 Has Fathers4Justice been successful as a pressure group?
2 Why is the Countryside Alliance an outsider group?
3 What pressure group methods is the Church of England using in its no change to marriage campaign?
4 How did Kony 2012 attract worldwide attention?
5 What is the pressure group status of the Stop the War campaign?

Answers on p.111

Exam practice

Examine the extent to which the internet has changed the way in which citizens can make their voice heard and take part in the democratic process. **(10 marks)**

Answers and quick quiz online

> **Examiner tip**
>
> This question is asking for your views about the impact of the internet on a citizen's participation in the democratic process. To gain high level marks you will need to include case studies.
>
> A possible plan for an answer could be:
>
> - Describe what is meant by the phrase 'the internet', mentioning social media like Twitter, the ability to have 24-hours news freely available from across the world and the use of YouTube to show almost instant photos or film.
>
> - The ways the internet has given empowerment to citizens: the recent conflicts in the Middle East where journalists are not allowed but 'citizen journalists' are using the internet to tell their story; campaigns like Kony that started as an internet campaign; in the UK, a website called 38degrees that hosts a variety of campaigns was successful in halting the sale of publicly owned forests; the government has introduced e-petitioning allowing the public to put forward ideas for parliamentary debate.
>
> - Finish with concluding comments on the benefits and possible drawbacks of the internet for participation.

Chapter 13 Active citizenship skills and participation

Becoming an informed citizen, a participating citizen, and an active citizen

Overview
Revised ☐

By using your Active Citizenship Profile and your knowledge of the active citizenship work that you have undertaken, you should be prepared to answer the question set in Section B of Unit 2: Democracy and Active Citizenship Participation. It is important that you take your Active Citizenship Profile with you into the examination room as you are allowed to refer to your Profile when answering questions.

Section B of this examination paper accounts for 40 per cent of the total marks available for the AS qualification. The aim of this section of the course is for you to be able to demonstrate your own knowledge of participation and understanding of active citizenship.

Each question on each of the units is assessed by awarding marks for each assessment objective. The Assessment Objective that assesses your active citizenship participation is AO3, which also assesses your ability to communicate using suitable citizenship terminology.

Examiner tip

Most of the marks awarded for the Section B questions relate to AO3: writing and communicating about taking action. A limited number of marks are awarded for the ability to evaluate (AO2).

Therefore the key to achieving good results is to understand about taking action in a citizenship context and being able to explain aims, methods and achievement or reasons for lack of success. This both relates to your own activities and those of others you have studied.

Understanding the basics
Revised ☐

The Active Citizenship Profile indicates three levels of citizen involvement and participation:

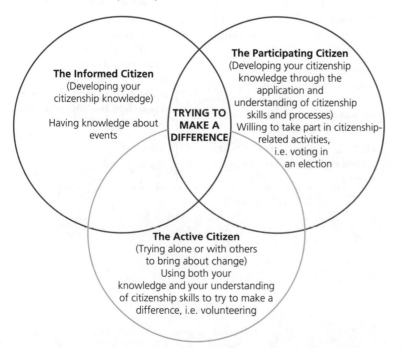

The Informed Citizen
(Developing your citizenship knowledge)

Having knowledge about events

TRYING TO MAKE A DIFFERENCE

The Participating Citizen
(Developing your citizenship knowledge through the application and understanding of citizenship skills and processes)
Willing to take part in citizenship-related activities, i.e. voting in an election

The Active Citizen
(Trying alone or with others to bring about change)
Using both your knowledge and your understanding of citizenship skills to try to make a difference, i.e. volunteering

Now test yourself

Which types of citizen participation fit the following scenarios?

1 Doing some internet research
2 Drafting a questionnaire
3 Meeting your local councillor to discuss an issue
4 Writing to your MP
5 Helping out at a local charity shop

Answers on p.111

You should have recorded in your Active Citizenship Profile details of your active citizenship involvement since the beginning of the course. Remember that your active citizenship record also involves any activities relating to CIST 1 (Unit 1) of the AS course. The more detail you record in your Profile the more helpful it may be when answering questions in the examination. It may also include work you undertake in the community.

The Active Citizenship Profile

Revised

Ensure that you are only using the profile that your centre has downloaded from the AQA website (www.aqa.org.uk). The profile can be handwritten or maintained on a computer and printed out to take into the examination. The profile is divided into three parts, one relating to each of our types of citizenship participation.

Scenario One

Your class decides to arrange for a representative of Amnesty International to visit the class and lead a discussion about Human Rights whilst you are studying CIST 1. Below is a diary that might be kept to support the work that was undertaken.

A Developing your own knowledge

Start date and completion date	Content area	Nature of the task	Evidence	Reflection
3/10 – 24/10	Human Rights CIST 1	Researching Human Rights and the work of Amnesty International	The class was split into four groups and each reported back to the class and shared their materials. My group researched the European Court of Human Rights; its origins, make up and how it makes decisions. We also researched the UK case about prisoners and voting. On 16/11 we made a PowerPoint presentation to the class of our findings.	It was an interesting piece of research as we had read reports about the ECHR in the tabloid newspapers and felt we had a better understanding after doing our research of the ways in which the court works.

B Applying your knowledge through citizenship skills

Start date and completion date	Content area	Nature of the task	Evidence	Reflection
18/11–25/11	Organising a debate about Human Rights	A class discussion took place on 18/11 where we agreed to invite a speaker from Amnesty International to discuss Human Rights especially in regard to the HRA(1998).	I was asked to chair the event. The class decided who would invite the speaker and clear the talk with the Head of Sixth. The room layout was agreed and the class was split into two groups each taking a differing viewpoint about the HRA and the need to reform the Act. We decided that one person would also record the discussion so we could watch the event later. Students were asked to go away and carry our further research and submit written questions to me.	I was pleased to be asked to chair the event and felt I needed to do some extra research as the questions were submitted so I had a handle on the topic being raised.

C Participating to bring about change

Start date and completion date	Content area	Nature of the task	Evidence	Reflection
3/12–5/12	Debate about Human Rights	Class debate featuring a speaker from Amnesty International	As well as the film of the event, we invited the local press who took a photo and printed an article. Having clearly structured the debate following the talk by the Speaker, the event went very smoothly. Some of the group organised a post-talk evaluation questionnaire.	The results of the questionnaire showed that the group had a clear understanding of the nature and workings of the HRA as well as how the ECHR works. I think I have gained in confidence from Chairing the event and felt better informed about the issues relating to Human Rights. All the hand-outs, PowerPoints and the case studies from Amnesty will help me prepare for the examination.

Scenario Two

I am investigating a local issue.

In my neighbourhood there is a major problem with litter.

A Developing your own knowledge

Start date and completion date	Content area	Nature of the task	Evidence	Reflection
13/2–1/3	Citizenship in Action CIST2	Discussions with my friends and neighbours about the extent of litter in our local area.	Following meeting my friends and discussing the problem I decided to collect some evidence and went out and took photos of the litter left lying around. I researched issues relating to litter on the internet and researched the work of 'Keep Britain Tidy' and found out that my local council was responsible for litter collection.	I enjoyed doing my research as it helped me understand whom I had to approach to try to resolve the problem.

B Applying your knowledge through citizenship skills

Start date and completion date	Content area	Nature of the task	Evidence	Reflection
5/3–18/3	Citizenship in Action CIST 2	Deciding how to apply pressure to bring about a change.\n\nI decided after taking my photos to write a report and submit it to the local council hoping they would take some action.\n\nI discovered that most of the litter arose at the weekend and was associated with several fast food shops in the area.	I produced a written report and included some of my photos. I also got a petition together asking the local council to take some action. I went out with my friends and we got 250 local residents to sign our petition.	I really enjoyed this work and enjoyed meeting local people.\n\nMany people said it was about time that something was done about the litter.\n\nI had to make sure that my report and the petition was really based upon evidence that could be proven.

C Participating to bring about change

Start date and completion date	Content area	Nature of the task	Evidence	Reflection
25/3	Citizenship in Action CIST2	Arranging a meeting with my local councillor.\n\nIn my research I found that I had three local councillors for my area. I wrote to each of them and asked to meet them to discuss the issue. All three agreed and we met locally and I presented them with my petition and report.	The councillors contacted the local press and an article and photo appeared in the local paper.\n\nThe council agreed to discuss the issue and I was invited to attend.\n\nAs a result of my campaign the local shop keepers and the council have agreed to fund some more waste bins in the area and ensure they are emptied on Mondays.	I never thought that I could bring about a change. But thanks to my friends and my neighbours we were able together to solve the problem.\n\nI now feel I have the confidence and skills to help to solve other problems.

> **Examiner tip**
>
> Before the exam, remember to review what you have written in your profile to ensure it is up to date, that what you wrote at the beginning of the course now reflects your greater understanding of the nature of Active Citizenship work and that you can apply correct citizenship terminology to what you have undertaken.

> **Examiner tip**
>
> Remember that you should also include examples of your active citizenship participation where appropriate when answering questions for Unit 2: Section B.

Using your profile in the examination

Section B of the CIST2 question paper comprises questions 5 to 8. This section of the paper is worth 60 of the 90 marks available for the unit and of those 60 marks, 54 are AO3 marks (Communication and Action).

Question number	Description of question	Marks given
Q5	Relate to work you have done, so you should use material from your profile.	5 marks
Q6	Relate to work you have done, so you should use material from your profile.	15 marks
Q7	This question is supported by stimulus material, and relates to a context where you could make reference to your own activities and use evidence from your profile where appropriate.	15 marks
Q8	This question requires a traditional essay answer and again you should be able to make reference to your own active citizenship work. This may relate to research you have undertaken as well as complete Active Citizenship tasks.	25 marks

Exam practice

Sample questions and using your profile.

5 Identify two pieces of research you had to undertake as a part of Active Citizenship tasks   **(5 marks)**

> You just need to state some research that you have undertaken and ensure it is linked to an Active Citizenship Task. What elements of the profiles above would you use to answer this question?

6 Explain how working with others can make a difference when undertaking active citizenship tasks.   **(15 marks)**

> You need to refer to work undertaken that involved working with others, research, investigation, taking action. You also need to explain the benefits of working with others. These benefits should relate to the desired outcomes of the activity. What elements of the Profile above would you use to answer this question?

7 Source

Many people feel the press are too influential and in regard to many political decisions they seem to set the agenda.

To what extent should we be concerned about the power and influence of the press in the UK?   **(15 marks)**

> This question is about the power of the press so any comments on other forms of the media need to be placed in context. Mention can be made of the role of local, regional and the national press. Specific case studies would strengthen the response. Whilst a conclusion should be drawn there is no set conclusion when answering a question of this nature. What elements of the Profile above would you use to answer this question?

8 Why don't more citizens get involved in campaigning about local issues? Discuss   **(25 marks)**

> The response can refer to local issues you are aware of, in a general sense, or relate to work you may have undertaken in your own local community. What elements of the Profile above would you use to answer this question?

Answers and quick quiz online

Online

Examiner tip

If timing is an issue for you, consider answering this examination paper in reverse order so if you are running short on time you are doing so on questions which have fewer marks. Remember Q8 is worth 25 of the 90 marks for the whole paper.

Examiner tip

Remember that case studies of your own active participation should be used when answering questions in any of the examination papers.

You may have been involved in some of the following activities during the course which should be included in your profile and add an AO3 dimension to any answers you write:

- researched issues and made presentation to others
- taken part in discussions or formal debates
- taken part in the Bar Council competition
- visited a Magistrates' or Crown Court
- met with outside visitors to your class
- carried out surveys in the local community
- met with local or national politicians
- attended local council meetings.

Answers

Chapter 1

1.1 What is a citizen?

1 A **citizen** is a member of a country with certain protections in the form of rights.

   A **subject** describes a person living under a system of monarchy.

2 Active citizenship means taking an active role in the country in which a citizen lives.

3 People have different ideas about the extent to which citizens have responsibilities to the community around them and/or have obligations to be actively contributing to it, e.g. individualist v. communitarian.

4 **Civil**: Right to fair trial

   Political: Right to vote

   Social: Right to education.

1.2 Is there agreement about what 'being British' means?

1 Any two of the following:
   ● British Overseas Territories Citizenship (BOTC)
   ● British Citizen
   ● Types of citizenship status for peoples in former colony countries
   ● Dual citizenship

2 ● Being born in the UK
   ● Adoption
   ● By descent
   ● Registration
   ● Via naturalisation

3 ● Colonial history means there are many overseas citizens with varied cultures.
   ● Varied cultures, ethnicities and religions are practised in Britain.
   ● Britain is made up of four nations (England, Scotland, Wales and Northern Ireland).
   ● There are cultural differences between the regions of each nation (e.g. Northern England and Southern England).

4 ● Symbols
   ● Language or dialect
   ● Personal beliefs (for example, whether or not they support the monarchy).

1.3 How do individuals and groups define their identity/identities and where are these definitions drawn from?

1 Any two of the following:
   ● Regionality
   ● Ethnicity
   ● Religion
   ● Age
   ● Gender
   ● Nationality
   ● Employment

2 Primary socialisation is the stage a person learns interaction like language, trust and affection and the values and norms particular to their family.

   Secondary socialisation occurs when a person begins to communicate with those outside the family and is exposed to the norms and values of wider society.

3 Some theorists believe that social classes have begun to merge as salaries improved along with working conditions, life chances and education.

4 Citizenship concerns the communities that citizens live within and it is these communities that impact and form individual identities.

Chapter 2

2.1 How much change and continuity is there in migration patterns?

1 **Push:** famine, war, natural disasters and persecution.

   Pull: living conditions, employment, study and family

2 **Against:** population rise, strain on resources and services, cultural conflict and fewer jobs for indigenous population.

   For: fills skills shortages, the state does not have to pay for education of migrant workers and net migration may not always rise.

3 ● Mass movement of people after Second World War
   ● Recruitment of workers after Second World War
   ● Indian independence from Britain in 1947
   ● Membership an enlargement of European Union.

4 Australia.

2.2 How far can Britain be described as a multicultural society?

1 Multiculturalism attaches importance to diversity and celebration of different cultural identities, whereas the assimilation model requires different cultures to merge into the 'host' or dominant culture. Collective cultural identity is given preference to individual cultural identity.

2 As a busy dock, London has a long history of immigration. It is an attractive destination as it has a wide range of jobs, opportunities, housing, schools and universities.

3 Urban areas tend to have a greater chance of employment and education and therefore more likely to attract migrants.

4 Any of the following:
   ● resentment over migrant workers
   ● lack of ethnic integration
   ● increases in race- related crime and violence and
   ● differences between what is considered legal and illegal in different countries.

2.3 What is stereotyping?

1 Any of the following:
- By exaggerating aspects of their cultural identity.
- By 'tagging' or labelling individuals or groups in society
- Examples might be: 'women are bad drivers', 'young people wearing hooded tops are trouble-makers'.

2 Stereotyping may be caused by:
- An unconscious function to simplify the world around us.
- Dominant groups in society attempting to suppress others.
- Existing prejudice
- Media influence

3 - By creating fictional characters in soap operas, advertising and TV shows which are based on stereotypes.
- By 'over-reporting' stories which portray certain groups in a negative light.

4 **Pluralist model** suggests that the media reflect the content that the public demand but presumes that the public are not influenced by media they read and source information and entertainment from a range of sources.

Cultural dominance model suggests that a small social group dominates the media industry and therefore the media tend to reflect their bias. However, many believe that as those from a variety of social and cultural backgrounds are now able to work in the industry, one cultural group no longer dominates.

Marxist/manipulative model suggests that the media is a way of controlling the less powerful or wealthy in society but fails to appreciate the public's ability to analyse information or the rise and dominance of new media.

Chapter 3

3.1 Prejudice and discrimination

1 **Indirect discrimination** describes a situation in which someone is unintentionally and/or indirectly treated differently.

Direct discrimination describes a situation in which someone is intentionally and/or directly treated differently.

Positive discrimination is treating someone differently to improve their situation

Negative discrimination is treating someone differently to harm or restrict their situation.

2 **Prejudice** describes beliefs that a group or individual hold and discrimination describes actions based on prejudiced beliefs.

3 **Genocide** is discrimination on a much wider scale, involving a large group of people; it is characterised by extreme forms of violence in an attempt to destroy an entire national or racial group.

4 Any of the following:
- Stereotypes
- Irrational fear
- Personal preference
- Experience.

3.2 Disadvantage: how are life chances distributed among different social groups?

1 Being able to access quality education at all levels may affect an individual's ability to gain future employment and higher wages. Lack of employment opportunities will directly impact an individual's income and consequently their quality of life.

2

It is a meritocracy because ...	It is NOT a meritocracy because ...
Education, healthcare and employment are available to all citizens and the law protects them from being discriminated against by the state/employers.	Instances of discrimination do still exist and citizens do not all enjoy the same levels of equality in: • healthcare (some can afford private healthcare) • education (areas differ in the quality of education available and some can afford private schooling). • employment (some areas in the UK have more employment opportunities than others)

3 **Social class** can affect life chances because the children of those in higher social classes tend to remain in higher social classes regardless of educational achievement.

Gender affects life chances because women live longer than men but on average have lower salaries because they are often restricted by part-time and lower paid jobs because of the expectation that they have the main responsibility for childcare.

4 Any three of the following:

Sexuality – homophobic bullying or discrimination can drastically affect an individual's mental health and future opportunities.

Age – the elderly are more likely to live on low incomes as they are reliant on pension payments. However, there are more elderly people than ever before; and they are the age group most likely to vote in elections so this may mean they are a group with growing influence.

Disability – disabled people are less likely than able bodied people to be in full-time education, employment or training and consequently earn less than able bodied people who have the same qualifications or training. However, arguably attitudes are changing and modern legislation protects disabled people from discrimination.

Ethnicity – in some respects, minority ethnic groups may have been disadvantaged financially due to migration, but some ethnic groups (Caribbeans, Black Africans, Indians and Chinese) experience greater social mobility than their white counterparts, which is thought to be due to educational achievement.

3.3 To what extent does poverty exist in Britain?

1 - There are different definitions of poverty: relative poverty or absolute poverty.
- Levels of poverty can vary drastically between more and less economically developed countries.

2 A group in society who, over generations, are excluded from normal society because they are either unable to break the poverty cycle or are vulnerable and isolated or are criminal.

3 There is much debate about the causes of poverty in the UK. Answers may discuss any of the following (but this table is not exhaustive):

Low income families – some believe that certain groups are trapped in low-paid work and subsequent poverty whereas others believe that any individual can better their chances of higher paid work via education and hard work.

Location – although many accept that certain parts of the UK have suffered greater unemployment than others, there are those who argue that families/individuals should move or commute to areas with better employment opportunities.

Culture – some believe that for many families, lack of interest in education has led to a culture of low-paid work or unemployment over several generations. However, others believe that such families have poor educational opportunities and are prevented from succeeding due to barriers to education (i.e. low income limits funds to travel to college, etc., and access to books and the internet).

4 Some argue we should disregard poverty as a term and focus on those groups who are on the lowest incomes in society.

Chapter 4

4.1 What steps can government take to reduce discrimination and disadvantage?

1 It means that, as far as possible, everyone should be treated fairly.

2 It is often subtle and unintentional – this can make it harder to identify and prove.

3 Any three of the following:

Equal Pay Act 1970 – ensures men and women are paid equal amounts for the same job.

Sex Discrimination Act 1975 – protects men and women from discrimination on the grounds of their sex or because they are married.

Race Relations Act 1976 – prevents discrimination on the grounds of race.

Equality Act 2006 – prevents discrimination on the basis of age; disability; gender; proposed, commenced or completed gender reassignment; race; religion or belief and sexual orientation.

New Deal – this policy offered financial support and help to those citizens who were actively seeking employment, to help them find and keep a job.

Minimum wage – this policy meant most workers are entitled to a national minimum level of pay to protect vulnerable groups in low income roles.

4 The Equality and Human Rights Commission (EHRC) promotes the interests of groups that may face hurdles to equal opportunities, and informs the public on these issues. It provides legal advice to companies on how to promote equal opportunities, and to employees that feel they have been unfairly treated and publishes reports on specific areas of discrimination.

4.2 How effective have anti-discrimination policies been?

1 Any two of the answers below:

Main strengths – an employer or public body can be prosecuted if they breach current discrimination legislation; there is substantial case history which can be used to help to identify cases of discrimination; when prosecutions are successful it sends a clear warning that discrimination will not be tolerated; legislation can change attitudes over time.

Main weaknesses – establishing discrimination can be difficult and open to interpretation; indirect discrimination may occur without an individual realising it; many people feel daunted about challenging an employer or public body; employers may give other reasons/excuses for discriminatory behaviour; challenging people's long-standing prejudices can be difficult.

2 ● Success is dependent on individuals prosecuting cases of discrimination. This can be stressful, time consuming and expensive.

● Proving discrimination may be difficult.

● Existing prejudices may be difficult to break down.

3 The existence of the legislation itself is a sign that society does not accept discrimination. Successful cases prosecuted against employers or public bodies, using the legislation, show the rest of society that discrimination will not be tolerated. Employers and public bodies are then likely to change existing policies to ensure that they are not in danger of discriminating against groups or individuals in the light of such case histories.

Chapter 5

5.1 Concept of a 'right' and the relationship between rights and duties

1 Legal rights come from specific statutes, laws made by Parliament.

2 A legal system is defined by the following principles: it is binding on the whole of society; it reflects the moral attitudes of society; it evolves to reflect changing moral values; it punishes people who commit criminal offences; it ensures contracts between people/companies are honoured.

3 **Relative duties** – duties that have a corresponding right, e.g. the duty to pay a debt has a corresponding right for a person to be paid what is owed to them.

Absolute duties – duties that do not have a corresponding right, e.g. the duty of a citizen not to break the law.

4 What is the difference between a claim right and a liberty right?

A **claim right** is one which infers a corresponding duty to the right-holder but a **liberty right** is a 'freedom' or permission to do something.

5.2 Different types of rights

1 This list is not exhaustive but any of the following are valid:

Right to vote – Representation of the People Act, 1969

Right to free education or training until the age of eighteen – Education Act 1944 and subsequent Education Acts

Right to practise religion – Human Rights Act, 1998

Right to a fair trial – Human Rights Act, 1998

2 The law is described as dynamic because it adapts to changing social, economic and political factors.

3 There are many examples that may be used, the example below is from the text:

A mother's right to know about any medical treatment her fifteen-year-old daughter is receiving (for example, the contraceptive pill) conflicts with that daughter's right to privacy or confidentiality.

4 A citizen may resolve conflicting rights with the other party involved via negotiation or mediation of some kind but they may also use the court system to resolve conflicting rights.

Chapter 6

6.1 Human rights

1 **A constitution** contains the rules of government and the rights of citizens; it can be codified (i.e. written down in a single document) or uncodified (i.e. contained in several different documents, laws or customs).

Parliamentary sovereignty is the principle that parliament is the supreme law maker.

2 The human rights abuses of the Second World War and in particular the Holocaust.

3 Some people felt that although the ECHR existed, it was time-consuming and expensive to seek redress under the ECHR. The HRA meant that the ECHR was now part of UK law and so judges in the UK could apply the convention.

4 There are many arguments against the creation of the HRA. This list is not exhaustive. The following are common arguments against the HRA:

● Citizens enjoyed rights in many countries before the ECHR was created and the Human Rights Act is not entrenched and could be repealed at any time.

● Countries are still allowed to stray from their obligations to carry out most of the rights in times of emergency.

● HRA gives too much power to judges that must interpret it, possibly causing conflict between Parliament and the Courts.

● The HRA should not apply to all because some people in society should not be entitled to all of their rights, i.e. convicted criminals.

● The ECHR is not drafted in the same way as UK statute. European legislation is drafted in wider terms, whereas UK statute tends to be more detailed. This leads to variations in how it is interpreted in different European countries.

6.2 The right to know

1 The DPA aimed to protect the information held on an individual and allow access to a person's information if they requested it.

2 The FOIA aimed to ensure that citizens could ask public authorities if they held any information on a particular subject; and to achieve more transparency in terms of government activities.

3 The right to know allows citizens to know about the decisions that government are making, and publicise/criticise them.

4 A public authority may withhold information if:

● the information is too sensitive in terms of national security or relations with other countries

● the request is unnecessary as the information will be, or is already published

● the request would cost too many man hours/much money to supply the information

● the request is vexatious (has been made before or is being made to waste time)

● the information requested is legally privileged, for example communications between the Queen and Government are confidential.

● the request concerns personal information or commercial confidences.

6.3 Other rights of UK citizens

1 The provision for welfare rights is created by various complex statues and delegated legislation.

2 A government that abolished the welfare state would be very unpopular and risks being voted out of power.

3 It is assumed that if a defendant has indeed acted in self-defence then this can be claimed as a legal defence during a criminal court case.

4 The right to a fair trial is contained in the HRA and therefore in the most serious cases a jury is used. If juries were used in all criminal cases it would be incredibly expensive, time consuming and often unnecessary.

Chapter 7

7.1 Civil and criminal law

1 The main purpose of **criminal law** is to regulate and control society by punishing behaviour that society regards as wrong or unacceptable.

The main purpose of **civil law** is to allow citizens to seek a remedy through the courts if they are in dispute with another individual or company/organisation.

2 Criminal courts make decisions regarding guilt of a defendant and then pass sentence. Civil courts offer a decision as to whether the claim of the 'claimant' is valid and can award compensation.

3 Other differences include:

● Civil law is concerned with the individual v. another individual, a company or the state; criminal law is primarily concerns the state v. an individual.

● Criminal law: cases are usually heard in a Magistrates' Court or Crown Court; Civil law: cases are usually heard in Small Claims, County Court or High Court.

4 It is important that citizens can use civil courts to settle disputes about contracts and wills so they can have confidence that they will be fulfilled. If they didn't believe that they would be enforced/fulfilled then there would be little point in making them.

7.2 Legal representation

1 Answers may include:

● Many more solicitors than barristers.

● Different ways of working: solicitors in firms, barristers in chambers.

● Solicitors can sue clients to recoup their fees but barristers cannot.

- Barristers mainly work in higher courts and solicitors in Magistrates' Courts.

2 Having two legal professions allows for specialised advocacy and for legal professionals who have specialised in particular areas of law.

3 It is important that citizens have access to legal representation regardless of their financial situation as this would prevent their right to a fair trial and may mean that they are not able to present their defence properly. This is especially important in criminal cases as defendants may be facing a possible custodial sentence.

7.3 Alternative methods of resolving disputes

1 Alternative Dispute Resolution may be less expensive than litigation, less stressful, less confrontational, more private, less time consuming, more convenient and allow for decisions that satisfy both parties.

2 During mediation, the third party remains neutral and does not make any suggestions; however, during conciliation they play a more active role and during arbitration the decisions of the arbitrator can be binding.

3 Answers may include:
- Disputes between employers and employers surrounding pay, dismissal or discrimination.
- Disputes between an individual and a government department surrounding provision or a decision surrounding, for example, healthcare, education, asylum or pensions.

4 An ombudsman is an official who is appointed to check on government activity on behalf of an individual citizen and to investigate complaints that are made. This can be in a range of areas, e.g. health service, local government, legal services and housing.

Chapter 8

8.1 The role of the courts

1 This is the approach that courts take to try to interpret statutes. It means that they try to establish what purpose the statute intended to achieve.

2 Civil courts have the power to: award damages; to order that the terms of a contract are performed; to issue an injunction; to order that a contract be set aside; to amend documents to reflect the true agreement of the parties; and to clarify the law on a particular point.

3 Courts have to balance the rights of individual citizens, e.g. in owning property, making contracts and having personal privacy, with the responsibility of protecting the security of the state and its institutions, conserving resources and promoting public morality.

4 The **advantages of precedent** are that it allows for certainty, it gives clear practical rules because it is based on real cases and it allows evaluation of individual cases.

However, the **disadvantages of precedent** are that it creates a complex and voluminous system of case law which can be outdated. Precedents may be conflicting and the speed at which the law develops is dependent on cases being brought to court.

8.2 The courts and the Human Rights Act

1 Any relevant case study would gain credit from examiners. Case studies from the text are as below:

Thompson and Venables v News Group Newspapers Ltd (2001)

Two ten-year-old boys abducted, tortured and murdered a two-year old. They were convicted of his murder and served eight years in young offender units. The trial judge ordered injunctions to protect their identities being published. Several newspapers sought to lift the injunction citing a breach of Article 10 of the European Convention on Human Rights (right to freedom of expression). The court believed there was evidence that if the injunction were lifted the lives of Venables and Thompson would be at risk and the injunctions remained under Article 2 (right to life).

Douglas v Hello! Ltd (2001)

Catherine Zeta-Jones and Michael Douglas married in a hotel in New York and agreed a £1 million deal with OK! magazine to publish exclusive pictures of their wedding. Hello! Magazine managed to acquire photographs and published them. The couple argued that their right to privacy under the Human Rights Act had been breached. It was argued that the Human Rights Act did not apply to the case because Hello! magazine was not a public authority but the Court held that as the Court itself was a form of public authority it was therefore unable to ignore the provisions of the HRA. This meant that the original case was therefore able to succeed.

Othman v UK

Abu Qatada is a Jordanian citizen (also known as Omar Mahmoud Othman) who was granted asylum in the UK on grounds of religious persecution. He is an Islamic militant and believed by several governments to be involved in terrorism. He was imprisoned in the UK for suspected terrorist activity. The British Government then attempted to deport him to Jordan to face charges; however, Abu Qatada claims he will not receive a fair trial in Jordan and may face torture. The European Court of Human Rights ruled that it would be a breach of Article 6 (right to fair trial). Abu Qatada was therefore allowed to remain in the UK and released under strict bail conditions.

2 An individual could take a case to the European Court of Human Rights, an ombudsman or seek judicial review. In very specific circumstances they may seek the legal action of Habeas corpus whereby a citizen that has been unlawfully imprisoned can be seen in court.

3 The Human Rights Act allowed citizens to use any British court as a route to seek redress of a human rights breach, rather than having to use the European Court of Human Rights. It also means that British Courts can rule that an existing law is incompatible with the ECHR – meaning that Parliament will then have to change it.

4 The Supreme Court allowed the judiciary to be more separate from Parliament and therefore better ensures the right to a fair trial in cases against the state itself. The Supreme Court also gives clarity on how rights contained in the European Convention on Human Rights should be interpreted.

8.3 Judicial review

1 Judicial review allows a person who has been adversely affected by a decision of a public body to ask the court to

review the decision. Its purpose is to ensure that the rights of citizens are protected against the powers exercised by the state (via public bodies).

2 Judicial review can occur when an applicant has a sufficient interest in the matter to be reviewed and therefore has a close connection to the subject, and it does not concern a right protected by private law (arising from a contract or tort).

3 Remedies available through judicial review are:

   Damages – the payment of compensation.

   Injunction – an order preventing the defendant from some act.

   Declaration – a statement of the law and rights and responsibilities of the parties.

   Quashing Order which quashes the decision of a public body that has been called into question by judicial review.

   Mandatory Order which orders an inferior court or public body to do something.

   Prohibiting Order which prevents a tribunal or a public authority from doing something that could be subject to a quashing order. For example, it could be used to prevent a tribunal from starting proceedings that are outside of its jurisdiction.

4 Judicial review is **effective** because:

   ● It allows the citizen to question decisions made by government departments.

   ● It helps to protect the rights of citizens from the power of government.

   Judicial review is not effective because:

   ● The tests used for deciding whether a judicial review is unreasonable are too restrictive.

   ● Ascertaining the power of public bodies can be very difficult.

   ● Decisions that are the subject of judicial reviews often concern the politically motivated decision of a minister.

   ● If a judicial review concerns a matter of national security, courts are reluctant to assess the strength of evidence provided by the state or even consider whether decisions made were rational.

Chapter 9

9.1 The concept and nature of power

1 **Power** relates to the ability to make something happen due to your position i.e. economic, military or physical power. **Authority** relates to the ability to make things happen due to the legitimacy of your power, i.e. the police have the authority of the state as we as citizens have granted authority and power to the state on our behalf.

2 In theory Parliament holds ultimate power in the UK but many state that power resides within the 'core executive', the Prime Minister, ministers and advisors and senior civil servants, but Parliament has the power to dismiss a government, hold ministers to account and defeat proposed legislation.

3 **Devolution** is the transfer of powers from one body to another. It transfers power from a greater to a lesser body. In the case of the UK the term relates to the transfer of powers from the UK Parliament to the 'devolved bodies' of Scotland, Wales and Northern Ireland.

4 The leader of the Conservative Party has the ability to take the lead on policy matters and appoints their own shadow cabinet and cabinet when in government. The annual conference of the Conservative Party is not a policy-making body like those of the Labour and Liberal Democrats.

5 The term **mandate** is used to describe the ability of a political party to carry out its policies after winning an election in which they placed their manifesto (policy ideas) before the electorate.

9.2 Who has economic power in the UK?

1 A mixed economy is where ownership within the economy is divided between public (state) and private provision, i.e. in the UK the state provides a public health service (the NHS) but you can also purchase healthcare from the private sector. A free market economy is based upon the principle that all elements of the economy should be privately owned and the state should have limited involvement.

2 The state can intervene by taking ownership, i.e. during the banking crisis the government became the major shareholder in RBS and LloydsTSB. Traditionally the term 'nationalisation' is used to describe state ownership. The opposite position when the state sells its assets is called 'privatisation'. The state can intervene by raising or lowering taxes or interest rates to encourage or discourages growth or inflation.

   The state can encourage employment by setting up specific programmes or investing in public spending to encourage employment.

3 **Monetary policy** relates to the value of a currency and issues like inflation rates. **Fiscal policy** relates to how a government raises its income and its spending policies.

4 The financial sector in the UK, whilst being important to the UK economy and a major employer, is also a major international player in regards to banking and insurance, foreign exchange dealings and the London Stock Exchange.

5 The Monetary Policy Committee of the Bank of England, which independently of government meets each month to set the official UK rate of interest. It works within targets set by the UK government regarding inflation levels.

9.3 What is the influence of the media and how is its power controlled?

1 Daily national newspaper – the *Daily Telegraph*, radio – Heart, television – BBC.

2 Media ownership is an issue when there is a concentration of ownership within any one area or across several types of media. Most media companies now own a range of media platforms ranging from local newspapers to nationals, magazines, local radio, to television and digital services. The issues raised relate to lack of competition and choice for the public to the concentration of influence perceived to be held by those that own media interests. The recent case study of the attempt by News International to purchase the balance of shares it did not own in BSkyB indicates how seriously government takes this issue.

3 The *News of the World* campaigned in regard to the introduction of Sarah's Law whereby the police had to inform local communities about the whereabouts of sex offenders. Sarah's Law was proposed after the murder of eight-year-old Sarah Payne by a convicted sex offender.

4 **Agenda setting** means to be able to place a topic within the public arena that builds up a momentum so that other media develop the story and/or politicians become involved. An example is the way in which a number of newspapers portray actions by the European Union to create a negative perspective.

5 **Political spin** relates to the way in which politicians and their advisors attempt to place their own favourable interpretation upon a specific story, hoping that this aspect of the story will be used by the media.

Chapter 10

10.1 The nature of government and its impact on the lives of citizens

1 The United Kingdom does not have a written constitution or a codified constitution. The United Kingdom has an unwritten constitution made up of several elements and this provides a flexibility enabling elements to be changed to meet contemporary needs.

2 **Sovereignty** is defined as the ability for a state to have power over its peoples and to maintain the integrity of the state. The term 'parliamentary sovereignty' is often used to describe the belief in the absolute power of the UK Parliament above that of any other national or international body.

3 Examples could include: requirement to have your birth registered, involved in National Health Service provision, state supported nursery care and attended state schools.

4 A core element of existence for any state is that of the ability to defend itself and to devolve this to lesser bodies would in essence destroy the concept of national defence. On a practical level the costs and organisation involved can only be met at a national level. To have a group of different bodies within the UK deciding differing defence policies and priorities would not provide a coherent defence strategy.

5 To respect and obey the laws of the land. Others might include civic participation by voting or by serving on a jury.

10.2 Local democracy

1 Several types of local authority exist in England including: Parish/Town Councils, District Councils, County Councils and Unitary Authorities. In London there is the Grater London Authority and the London Boroughs.

2 Members of Parliament, directly elected Mayors, Police Commissioners, Councillors, Members of the devolved assemblies and Parliament.

3 The concept of a Unitary Authority is that within a given geographical area it is responsible for all local government services. In many parts of the country local government operates within a two- or three-tier structure. In some areas there are Parish Councils with limited powers, District Councils with limited powers and more powerful County Councils.

4 If a council operates outside its legal authority it is deemed to be acting in *ultra vires*. If this is proven individual councillors can be ordered to pay any costs involved in acting outside their powers.

5 Stand for election to the local authority and join a local pressure group.

10.3 What is the impact of the EU on life in the UK?

1 The UK joined the European Economic Community in 1973

2 This was a major European Union Treaty which introduced ideas like the Social Chapter and allowed for countries to opt out of some developments.

3 The Conservative Party belongs to the European Conservatives and Reformist Group, the Labour Party belongs to the Socialist Group, the Liberal Democrats belong to the Group of Alliance of Liberals and Democrats for Europe.

4 Where states work together within an international body. Each state has equal powers and can opt out of any decision.

5 Over recent years each European Treaty has increased the powers of the European Parliament.

Chapter 11

11.1 What does 'taking part in the democratic process' mean?

1 In its purest form the phrase relates 'people-power'. Today we use the term to describe a form of government where there are free and fair elections where the people can hold those elected to account at regular elections.

2 The term direct democracy is where the people make decisions and where ultimate powers reside with the people. In the UK referendums are a form of direct democracy. Direct democracy also known as representative democracy, is where people are elected or appointed by the people to make decisions on their behalf.

3 The United Kingdom can be described as a democratic country as it has regular elections.

4 Whilst the membership of political parties is decreasing the number of people involved in the political process by their support of pressure groups and their use of e-media campaigning.

5 e-petitioning is an internet version of conventional petitioning where people sign up showing their support for a cause. The UK government introduced a system where citizens can set up their own petition and if they achieve the support of 100,000 others. Parliament may discuss the issue.

11.2 Citizens and the electoral process

1 Those who support the FPTP system claim one its benefits is that it is simple for the voter to understand and easy to count and arrive at a result.

2 Members of the Scottish Parliament are elected by the Additional Member System (AMS).

3 Electoral turnout relates to the number of people who actually vote as compared against the total number that could vote.

4 A Focus group is a way in which political parties and advertisers attempt to test ideas out on a representative group of citizens. They gather the people together and observe their reactions to set questions, views or opinions.

5 Police Commissioners are being elected using the Supplementary Vote (SV) system.

11.3 Do pressure groups improve the democratic process?

1 A pressure group is a group of concerned citizens who wish to influence others. They come together to promote their cause.

2 Insider status allows a pressure group or interest group to have access to those in power they may also be consulted by those in power.

3 A trade union like Unison can be classified as a multi cause group.

4 Taking part in a march is a form of direct action.

5 Think tanks are privately established policy-based bodies that seek to influence political and public policy. Many have close links with specific political parties.

Chapter 12

12.1 How do citizens bring about change?

1 An advantage of organising a march is that the public becomes aware of your cause, the media may report the event and your supporters are aware that others support the cause.

2 Owing to his celebrity status as both a well-known chef and a television personality, Jamie Oliver can achieve media coverage for the causes he wishes to support.

3 Martha used the internet to post details of her school meals. Within a short period of time she attracted thousands of supporters and achieved media coverage which boosted the number of her supporters.

4 Using Twitter on the internet to campaign enables people to post instant comments and gain worldwide coverage and supporters.

12.2 What are the key factors in successful campaigning?

1 A pressure group with a large membership can use its membership to campaign and promote its cause. Those in power, especially if they are elected, need to consider public opinion and if a large number of people are campaigning on an issue they need to consider all their views. A recent example of large membership campaigning was the successful campaign to stop the sale of publicly owned forests in the UK.

2 The media can assist a campaign by reporting its activities, ensuring that a wider audience is aware of the cause it is campaigning about.

3 Outsider status means that a pressure group doesn't seek support from those in power. It enables a group to freely campaign how it wishes.

4 The campaign organised via the website 38 degrees enabled those who wished to stop the sale of state-owned forests in the UK to gather support. It was successful because it brought together a wide range of groups opposed to the sale as well as gathering a vast number of individual supporters who lobbied their Members of Parliament.

5 Whilst the Stop the War campaign successfully organised a vast number of people to part in a national march they were unsuccessful in convincing sufficient Members of Parliament to ensure that the decision to go to war was overturned. It was also a politically motivated campaign that did not receive media support.

12.3 The impact of campaigns on political decision-making and political attitudes

1 Fathers4Justice has been very successful in raising the profile of issues concerned with parenting after a divorce, but has been unsuccessful in achieving any change in the law on the issue. Due to its campaigning methods it achieved a lot of media coverage, but the media turned against the group and it lost some support.

2 The Countryside Alliance was considered up to 2010 as an outsider group as the then Labour government did not support most of its aims and believed that those who supported the campaign were politically motivated against it.

What pressure group methods is the Church of England using in its no change to marriage campaign?

The Church of England gathered a petition to support its cause. It also campaigned in favour of its cause rather than against the proposed change in the law attempting to gather support for the current definition of marriage.

3 The Kony campaign gathered momentum due to the influence of the internet and social media.

4 The Stop the War campaign has outsider status as those in power do not support its aims.

Chapter 13

Becoming an informed citizen, a participating citizen and an active citizen

1 Doing some internet research

Internet research enables you to become an Informed Citizen.

2 Drafting a questionnaire uses skill and helps with understanding a process. It therefore helps you become a Participating Citizen. Carrying the task forward and organising the completion of the questionnaire and using the results to inform others would make someone an Active Citizen.

3 Organising a meeting with a local councillor and researching the questions to ask and then using the results to try to bring about change makes someone an Active Citizen.

4 Writing a letter to your MP is an example of being a Participating Citizen, using your knowledge and skills to raise an issue.

5 Volunteering is a form of Active Citizenship. Besides helping out, an Active Citizen undertakes this work to make a difference so it is important to realise what a difference your help would make to the charity concerned.